WATCHABLE BIRDS

OF THE ROCKY MOUNTAINS

Mary Taylor Gray

Photographs by Weldon Lee

Mountain Press Publishing Company
Missoula, Montana
1992

Third Printing, March 1997

Library of Congress Cataloging-in-Publication Data

Gray, Mary Taylor, 1955-
  Watchable birds of the Rocky Mountains / Mary Taylor Gray ;
photographs by Weldon Lee.
    p.   cm.
  Includes index.
  ISBN 0-87842-281-1 : $12.00
  1. Birds—Rocky Mountains. 2. Brid watching—Rocky
Mountains.
I. Lee, Weldon, 1937-   . II. Title.
QL683.R63G73   1992   92-10101
589' .0723478—dc20   CIP

Printed in Hong Kong by Mantec Production Company

MOUNTAIN PRESS PUBLISHING COMPANY
2016 Strand Avenue • P.O. Box 2399
Missoula, Montana 59806
(406) 728-1900

To Mom and Dad,
without whom nothing would have been possible.

— M. T. G.

Many thanks to Mike Carter of the
Colorado Bird Observatory for all his help.

WENDY SHATTIL

About the Author

Mary Taylor Gray is a professional wildlife and nature writer with three books and hundreds of magazine and newspaper articles to her credit. Her birdwatching column, "Words on Birds," appears monthly in the *Rocky Mountain News*. Mary holds a bachelor's degree in zoology, with an emphasis on animal behavior, and has taught summer nature writing workshops for the Rocky Mountain Nature Association. An avid hiker, camper, wildlife watcher, and conservationist, Mary lives in Denver, Colorado, with her two dogs, a cat, a horse, and many wild-bird neighbors for whom she buys lots of birdseed.

Contents

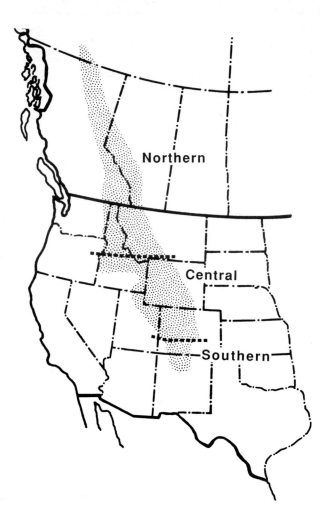

The Rocky Mountain region (stippled pattern). Labels and dashed lines mark boundaries of southern, central, and northern Rockies as discussed in this book.

Introduction

Have you ever noticed a brightly colored bird and asked, "What's that?" Or seen a bird spiraling and diving in the sky and wondered, "What's that bird doing?" If you've been charmed or intrigued by birds, would like to learn more about them, but don't consider yourself a "birdwatcher," then this book is for you.

Another bird guide? Not really. Most bird guides are geared for identification, offering a few terse facts and detailed descriptions that enable avid birders to distinguish among similar species. But most of us will never see birds from the closeup view of traditional bird guides. We see birds as we whiz by in a car or go for a walk in our neighborhood. We glimpse birds as they flutter among the trees, sit atop power poles or beg at our picnics. Figuring out the differences among five different species of brown sparrow is not our concern.

You won't find every bird in the west described in this book, nor even the most common or easily seen birds. Here you'll find a selection of "watchable" birds—those particularly noticeable and fun to watch because they're especially pretty, colorful, large or have interesting behaviors. We've included only those species the alert, nonbirdwatcher is likely to see.

Who is *Watchable Birds of the Rocky Mountains* for?

Written as much for the armchair naturalist as for the family on an outing, *Watchable Birds of the Rocky Mountains* goes beyond identification to reveal the "private lives" of our feathered friends. Here you'll discover the fun "personality" information about the birds around us, the tidbits of trivia that bring them to life.

This guide is designed for families, tourists, casual nature lovers and any person who enjoys birds and wildlife. For some it may be a first step toward an interest in birdwatching, for others merely a source of basic information and interesting trivia about the feathered inhabitants of our world. We've tried to give you a book that can be used as a companion to a field guide or that a family on a car trip in the Rocky Mountain West could read and enjoy even if they never actually see the bird they're reading about.

Now, go out and discover the *Watchable Birds of the Rocky Mountains*!

HOW TO USE THIS BOOK

Watchable Birds of the Rocky Mountains covers all or part of the states of New Mexico, Colorado, Wyoming, Montana, Idaho, Utah and the Canadian provinces of British Columbia and Alberta, overlapping into northern Canada. Mention is made of Alaska where ranges are appropriate.

The book is organized according to three basic habitats.

 Plains includes prairie grasslands, scrub and rangelands and old fields.

 Wetlands includes lakes, rivers, streams, ponds and marshes.

 Mountains covers foothills, canyons and mountain areas up through the alpine zone above timberline.

If you see a bird you want to identify, first ask yourself "Where am I?" based on the three habitats, then look for the bird in that chapter. The small drawing in the upper left corner of each bird description identifies the habitat. You can

Common Yellowthroat male

also use the guide to read up on the birds you'd expect to see in a certain area you're visiting. If you're headed to the mountains, you can check out what birds to keep an eye out for.

.Of course some habitats overlap. You may find yourself on the prairie along a cottonwood-lined stream or pond. Is this prairie or wetlands? Since the pond area qualifies as wetlands, look for your bird there.

For simplicity's sake we have "assigned" each bird to a habitat the species most often inhabits. But birds don't frequent these habitats exclusively. Don't be surprised if you see them somewhere else.

Plains and Mountains silhouette scale (top) and Wetlands silhouette scale (bottom) with arrows indicating size of bird in relation to familiar birds

Size: Familiar birds make up the two size silhouettes. For the Plains and Mountains the size silhouette features a hummingbird, sparrow, robin, crow, hawk and eagle; for Wetlands it shows a sparrow, robin, crow, duck, goose and pelican. An arrow indicates the size of each bird in relation to these familiar ones. Remember that body can't always be directly compared because birds are designed differently. A tall bird like the great blue heron has long legs and neck that make it appear large, yet its body is only the size of a duck, and it has the broad wingspan of a pelican! Birds also differ by profile—a hawk may be the size of a duck, but the hawk sits vertically and the duck horizontally. We have classified the size of each bird as closely as possible bearing in mind body size and the viewer's perception.

A.K.A. ("also known as") lists other common names for a particular bird, names that may be more familiar to you. The northern harrier, for example, has for years commonly been called the marsh hawk, and you may know gray jays better as camp robbers.

A brief description of the bird follows to help you identify it.

Natural History: gives you information on the bird and how it lives its life. Here you'll find fun and interesting facts, the "I didn't know that!" stuff.

White-tailed ptarmigan in winter plumage

When and Where to See Them: clues you to places to look at specific times of year. If months of the year are mentioned, they refer to the central Rockies. Adjust time slightly later the farther north you go, and earlier the farther south. Remember that migrating birds move north in the spring to their breeding grounds, and south in the fall to their wintering grounds. References to breeding and wintering ranges refer to these seasons. Resident birds live in the area year-round.

Eyecatchers: boxed at the bottom of the page, directs you to specific noticeable or outstanding features that will help you notice the species or distinguish it from other birds.

HOW TO WATCH BIRDS

Watching birds is lots more fun if you can identify them! A bird flits by and you think you noticed enough detail to identify it, but checking a bird guide you find ten different birds that might fit. Training yourself to make a few mental notes when you glimpse a bird will help your identification.

Size. It's difficult to accurately judge the size of birds at any distance. Instead, judge size in relation to birds you know. Is it about the size of a

Wood Duck male

sparrow? Is it bigger than a robin but smaller than a crow? To help you we've indicated size in relation to familiar birds on a silhouette chart.

Shape. What is the general shape? Is the bird round and chunky like a sparrow or slender like a nuthatch? Make note of the shape of body parts—wings, tail, bill, legs. Owls have round heads; great blue herons have very long legs; ducks have "duck bills." Magpies have distinct long tails and barn swallows have a forked "swallow tail." Falcons have slender, tapering wings for fast pursuit in the air, while hawks have wider wings for soaring.

Field Marks. Sometimes you only have a moment to glimpse a bird. Watch for noticeable features. Are there distinctive stripes, colors or patterns on the bird? Is the breast spotted, are there stripes over the eyes, or white edges to the tail? Do patches under the wings or on the tail "flash" when the bird flies? Does the bird have a crest like a Steller's jay or a kingfisher?

Posture/Position. Where you see a bird gives clues to its lifestyle. Is it gripping the trunk of a tree, perched on a tree limb, hopping on the ground or wading in the shallows? Also notice its posture. Is it sitting upright or holding its body parallel to the ground?

5

*Double-crested
Cormorant*

Voice. Birdsong fills the natural world with life and joyful music. Becoming familiar with a bird's song is not only a pleasure but an opportunity to learn who's in the neighborhood without even seeing them!

Habitat. Don't just note what a bird looks like. Figuring out where it lives will give you clues to its identity. Are you in a woodland or meadow or is the bird close to, or in, water?

WILDLIFE WATCHING: ETHICS AND ETIQUETTE

When watching birds remember that you are in essence entering the animals' "home" and should conduct yourself as a guest. Respect the animals and don't disturb them, their nests or their habitat. Don't approach any closer than the birds feel comfortable. If they alter their behavior, stop feeding or otherwise seem agitated, back off. Never chase, feed, handle or disturb animals. When you go out birdwatching, leave your pets at home.

We've all seen closeup photos of hawks or eagles with the bird puffed up in a threatening posture, its beak open in a threat gesture. That photographer approached too close and threatened the bird. Intrusion into a bird's living space can expose it to predation, keep it from feeding or other essential activities, or cause it to leave or abandon its nest, exposing eggs or chicks to predation or the elements.

No photo or viewing opportunity is worth harassing or stressing wildlife. In appreciating and watching birds and other wildlife, we have a responsibility to protect and preserve the animals that share our world.

Canada goose swimming with gosling

Birds of the Plains

Swainson's Hawk
Red-tailed Hawk
Ferruginous Hawk
American Kestrel
Ring-necked Pheasant
Sharp-tailed Grouse
Mourning Dove
Great Horned Owl
Burrowing Owl
Downy Woodpecker
Northern Flicker
Western Kingbird
Horned Lark
Barn Swallow
Black-billed Magpie
American Crow
Black-capped Chickadee
American Robin
Lark Bunting
Western Meadowlark
Bullock's Oriole
House Finch

Swainson's Hawk

Buteo swainsoni
Family: Hawk

A.K.A. Prairie hawk, gopher hawk, prairie buzzard, grasshopper hawk

The Swainson's is a fairly large hawk with dark head, back and wings, light breast and underside, white chin and a reddish brown bib across the neck and upper chest.

Natural History: The Swainson's hawk is a bird of the open country. It patrols its grassland home, cruising slowly above a field or meadow on wings tipped slightly up, circling as it watches the ground for a movement that signals a meal. The Swainson's may sit atop a fencepost or other low vantage point awaiting opportunity, transforming to a lightning-fast predator as it snatches up meadow mice, gophers, grasshoppers and other insects.

Swainson's hawks have been reported hunting in rather unorthodox ways— waiting on the ground at an animal burrow till the hapless creature ventures above ground, to be nabbed by the waiting hawk; hopping about among the grass and scrub snapping up grasshoppers and other insects; or grabbing flying insects with their talons while on the wing, then reaching down to "eat from the hand" while still in flight.

The Swainson's is a familiar roadside hawk, hanging out on fenceposts and telephone poles and not particularly disturbed by passing traffic. Unfortunately this habit amongst Swainson's and other roadside hawks leads to lots of "sport" shootings by passing trigger-happy motorists, a pasttime strictly illegal, since raptors are protected under federal law.

When and Where to See Them: In open grasslands, shrublands, prairies and deserts into the lower mountains, Swainson's is a common summer hawk throughout the Rockies, migrating to South America in winter. They may appear above timberline during migration and after nesting.

EYECATCHERS

Look for the rusty-brown bib of this large hawk. In flight the wing linings are lighter than the outer flight feathers, and it holds its wings tipped up above the horizontal when gliding.

Swainson's Hawk photographed at the Rocky Mountain Raptor Program, Colorado State University—a rehabilitation center for injured raptors in Fort Collins, Colorado. This bird has since been released to the wild.

Red-tailed Hawk
A.K.A. Red-tail, hen hawk

Buteo jamaicensis
Family: Hawk

A big, brown hawk with a noticeably reddish tail and dark bars on the front of the wings, the red-tail comes in several color phases that can make identification confusing. The more common light phase is buff colored underneath with reddish streaking, while the dark phases have a uniformly brown body. Immature hawks lack the red tail.

Natural History: Circling lazily on the thermals or sitting in state upon a telephone pole, the red-tailed hawk is a handsome and familiar friend. The most common hawk in America, the red-tail's wide distribution has fostered a phrase for birdwatchers trying to identify hawks—"If all else fails, it's a red-tail."

A big hawk with a chunky body, broad wings and wide tail, red-tails are frequent prairie landmarks, almost a part of the blue western sky as they soar, sometimes hanging motionless against the breeze on outstretched wings. In early morning they flap slowly up, up in the cool air. Then as the air warms and the thermals begin to rise, the broad-winged birds ride the rising air currents, sometimes several of them spiraling higher and higher till they become tiny specks. Not as fast as a falcon or one of the smaller birds of prey, the red-tail seems more deliberate in its hunting, hunting from the air or sometimes sitting atop a vantage point looking for prey with its telescopic eyes, then swooping down on a meal.

During courtship the red-tail pair spirals in the air, crossing each other's path, the male circling behind and above the female, sometimes flying straight down at her, touching or grasping her talons.

Red-tails typically nest in the crotch of a large tree where they have a good view, building a bulky, platform nest of sticks, lining the nest cup with bark and leaves.

When and Where to See Them: In open wooded areas, plains and scrublands into foothills areas. Red-tails are resident in the south and central Rockies, moving throughout the Rockies into northern Canada for nesting in spring, summer and fall.

EYECATCHERS

The savage scream of the red-tailed hawk may announce its presence in the area before you see it circling overhead. This large brown hawk's red tail is especially noticeable in flight with the light behind it.

Red-tailed Hawk photographed at the Rocky Mountain Raptor Program, Colorado State University—a rehabilitation center for injured raptors in Fort Collins, Colorado. This bird has since been released to the wild.

Ferruginous Hawk
A.K.A. Ferrug

Buteo regalis
Family: Hawk

One of the largest hawks, the adult ferruginous has two color phases. The common light phase has a reddish brown back, pale head and underside streaked with rufous-red. A dark V formed by the brown, fully feathered legs against the white body is visible in flight. The rare dark phase is reddish brown all over.

Natural History: Winter drives many raptors from the southern and central Rockies, but this is a time the big ferruginous hawk is easily seen as it haunts prairie dog towns looking for a meal. When the winter sun shines, bringing the dogs from their dens, the hawks come hunting, roosting atop telephone poles or other vantage points awaiting an opportunity to grab a rodent meal. The hawks sometimes hunt on the ground, landing atop a prairie dog mound just out of the rodent's line of vision, waiting for a dog to venture out, then grabbing it.

Ferruginous hawks prefer to build their nests in trees, but since these may be rare in their grassland habitat, the birds make use of what's available—a hillside or riverbank, bush or cliff edge. They line their coarse stick nests with dried yucca leaves, horse dung, weeds and roots. The hawks will drive competing predators like coyotes and great horned owls from their territory.

So important are prairie dogs and jackrabbits to this hawk that the number of nests built, eggs laid and young fledged is directly related to local small mammal populations. They are frequent roadside hawks, hanging out atop power poles along country roads, seemingly oblivious to passing vehicles.

When and Where to See Them: Ferruginous hawks haunt the grasslands and open areas of the southern and central Rockies year-round where there are large rodent populations. They extend their range in spring and summer into southern Canada.

EYECATCHERS

The "ferrug" is a large, reddish brown hawk with very light undersides, conspicuous as a winter hawk of the southern and central Rockies.

Ferruginous Hawk photographed at the Rocky Mountain Raptor Program, Colorado State University—a rehabilitation center for injured raptors in Fort Collins, Colorado. This bird has since been released to the wild.

American Kestrel

Falco sparverius

A.K.A. Sparrow hawk, mouse hawk, grasshopper hawk

Family: Falcon

A strikingly handsome, small falcon, the male has bright blue-gray wings, rusty red back with black barring, a peach-colored breast and a rufous-red tail. The female is similar to the male but her wings are rusty-brown, not blue. The crown of the head is blue-gray with a reddish spot. Both sexes have two vertical black streaks, called "whiskers," on the sides of the face.

Natural History: You've probably zoomed past a kestrel a thousand times in your car without knowing the bird perched on a roadside powerline was a sleek falcon. Seeing the kestrel is a treat, with its handsome, uniquely colored plumage, striking markings and dynamic behavior, all in a neat package no bigger than a robin. Like the burrowing owl, they're proof that birds of prey don't have to be big and macho to be fascinating.

Kestrels typically feed on grasshoppers and small mammals, abundant in the falcon's prairie habitat. They occasionally take small birds. Fleet and maneuverable, kestrels may hover motionless in the air on rapidly beating wings before swooping on their prey. Sometimes they cache prey in the grass to be eaten later. Used by falconers, kestrels were often flown at sparrows, hence their familiar name, sparrow hawk.

The kestrel is one of the most vocal raptors, rapidly sounding its *killy-killy-killy* call. When the female is on eggs or brooding young, the male will call her from the nest to feed her. Kestrels lay their eggs in treeholes, nooks and crannies of buildings and sometimes in magpie nests, using little if any nesting material. The male will sometimes sit on the eggs, an unusual habit among birds of prey.

When and Where to See Them: Many kestrels are resident birds in grasslands, parks and open areas at lower elevations in the southern and central Rockies, breeding into foothills elevations throughout the Rockies from spring through fall. They may appear above timberline after the nesting season.

EYECATCHERS

Perched on a power line, this little falcon might first be mistaken for a songbird by its upright posture, but its beautiful red and blue coloring and peachy breast soon identify it.

16

American Kestrel male photographed at the Rocky Mountain Raptor Program, Colorado State University—a rehabilitation center for injured raptors in Fort Collins, Colorado. This bird has since been released to the wild.

Ring-necked Pheasant
A.K.A. Chinese pheasant, Chinese ring-neck

Phasianus colchicus
Family: Grouse

A magnificent ground-dwelling bird with a plump body, the male ring-necked pheasant has a long, plumed tail and small greenish black head set on a skinny, white-banded neck. The male is very colorful, its golden body mottled with black. The eyes are surrounded by circles of naked red skin and the head has two small feathery tufts. By contrast the female is a nondescript brown with a shorter tail.

Natural History: The pheasant cock appears like a richly dressed sultan amongst his harem of drab, brown ladies. Carrying his emerald head and sweeping gold and black tail with hauteur, the male patrols his field and grassland habitat beneath our very noses, flushing in startled indignation when we accidentally stumble upon him. Flushed from the ground, the pheasant takes off in a whir of wingbeats. Its plump body sails just above the vegetation on short wings before landing again at a safe distance. Once it hits the ground the pheasant starts running to confuse any predator that might have marked its landing point. Its distinctive crow, sounding like a rusty gate opening under protest, is often heard across a meadow or stubblefield, though we may not see the actual bird. In the spring mating season the males compete among themselves for hens, crowing, fighting, spreading wings and tails and erecting the little feather tufts on their heads.

In winter the pheasant leaves its distinctive signature in the snow, sweeping a "snow angel" outline with its long tail, heavy body and short wings.

Certainly one of the most beautiful birds in the west, the pheasant is not a native but was introduced to the United States from China in the mid-1800s as a game bird and has made itself an important bird of grasslands and cultivated fields.

When and Where to See Them: Year-round in grasslands, open woodlands, brushy areas and agricultural fields of the central and northern Rockies into Canada.

EYECATCHERS

In the sunlight the pheasant cock's iridescent plumage shines green, purple, bronze, gold. Its long, sweeping tail and bright color make it a prince among birds. Startled from hiding, the pheasant flushes with a sudden flurry, flapping its wings furiously for a few moments before sailing across a field to land farther away.

Ring-necked Pheasant male

Sharp-tailed Grouse
Tympanuchus phasianellus

A.K.A. Sharptail
Family: Grouse

The sharptail is speckled brown and white with the typical plump body, long neck and small head of the chickenlike birds. True to its name, the sharp-tailed grouse has pointed tail feathers protruding from a wedge-shaped tail.

Natural History: Spring comes to the grasslands of the West and an age-old ritual is played out as sharp-tailed grouse and other wild chickens gather at ancestral dancing grounds, called leks, to perform their spring courtship dances.

The males dance to attract females and compete with other males. There is something compelling about the often comical gyrations of these plump, chickenlike birds. Flaring their wings, raising their pointed tails and lowering their heads till their bodies are nearly parallel to the ground, they stamp their feet rhythmically, turning this way and that like little wind-up toys, then jump in the air while beating their wings. Inflating the purple air sacs on their necks, they let out a resonant popping which may sound like wheezing bellows, cooing doves or a bubbling pool of mud.

Like so many of the wild chickens, sharptail populations have declined in many areas due to conversion of their grassland habitat to agriculture. The birds need tall grasses and shrubs for cover. Overgrazing by cattle, plowing of native prairie for cropland, and urban development have left the grouse and other grassland birds with greatly reduced habitat. The leks are ancestral, used year after year by succeeding generations. The birds remain faithful to these locations; once these breeding grounds are gone, the birds' reproduction cycle is disrupted. According to one story, a homestead was built on the site of a lek. When the birds arrived in spring to carry out their age-old dance, they found a house on their dancing grounds. Undiscouraged, they danced and performed on the roof of the house.

When it comes to bird showmanship, members of the grouse family are tops. Like sharptails, prairie-chickens and sage grouse are grassland residents that gather on leks in groups to perform spring courtship dances, booming and strutting for all they're worth. Ruffed and blue grouse, both forest-dwellers, perform alone. Ruffed grouse rapidly beat their cupped wings against the air, producing a drumming sound, while blue grouse perch on a stump and produce a resonant hooting from their purple air sacs.

When and Where to See Them: Sharptails are year-round residents of prairie grasslands throughout the northern plains from Colorado and Nebraska through northern Canada and Alaska. Grouse courtship dancing is highly watchable but occurs only in spring at very specific sites. Contact the wildlife agency in your area for more information.

EYECATCHERS

In flight, the pointed, wedge-shaped tail flashes white and is noticeably different from the fan tails of other grouse.

Sharp-tailed Grouse male

Male sharp-tailed grouse performing courtship display on lek

Mourning Dove

A.K.A. Turtledove, wood dove

Zenaida macroura

Family: Pigeon

This small-headed bird has gray-brown plumage that takes on a pinkish cast in some light, and an iridescent greenish-purple neck. Underparts are buffy. The long, spade-shaped tail has white edges very noticeable in flight. The dove is smaller than a pigeon.

Natural History: Mourning doves are pleasing and familiar friends—sitting side by side along telephone wires, cooing mournfully; striding about on the ground, their small heads bobbing back and forth; or flying up on whistling wings to roost, pretty spade-shaped tails spread to reveal white edges. In flight the mourning dove's small head, long tail and stubby wings form a stylized cross.

Mated doves seem affectionate pairs to human watchers, sitting close and cooing softly, leaning their heads against each other and rubbing necks with eyes closed. Though doves are the most heavily hunted game bird in North America, they maintain their numbers by nesting two to four times a year, laying two eggs in each clutch. Both parents sit on the eggs, the male pulling mostly day duty while the female takes the night shift.

The parents feed the young, called squabs, "pigeon milk"—regurgitated food from the crop of the adults, including material sluffed off of the stomach lining. Later the juveniles consume insects, worms and seeds.

When and Where to See Them: Year-round in fields, prairie woodlands, grassy meadows and city and suburban areas of the south and central Rockies, expanding in spring, summer and fall into southern Canada.

EYECATCHERS

This little brown dove, with its small head and long tail, is familiar from the way it walks—bobbing its head forward with each stride—how its wings whistle as it flies up to roost, and especially its sad, hooting *coo* that gives the bird its name.

Mourning Dove

Pair of mourning doves on a limb

Great Horned Owl

A.K.A. Hoot owl, cat owl

Bubo virginianus

Family: Owl

This large, round-headed owl displays two feathery tufts or "horns" on the head. It often looks like it has no neck. The plumage—brown with black barring—is very effective camouflage. This owl has large yellow eyes set in gold-colored facial disks.

Natural History: The great horned owl's barred, gray-brown plumage is such wonderful camouflage you've probably passed beneath one without any clue an owl roosted silently in a tree above you. Owls sit unmoving except for their round heads that swivel to follow movement, the great, "all-knowing" yellow eyes occasionally blinking sleepily.

Because of their nighttime habits and ability to hunt in the dark, many cultures have endowed owls with supernatural powers. Their hooting is a part of folklore, thought to be an omen or a message from the spirits. The owl's large eyes and omnipotent demeanor led many people to think the bird knew something they didn't, hence the adage "wise as an owl."

Whether or not you believe the owl is a spirit bird, it is a magnificent and effective night hunter. The great horned is such a fierce and voracious predator it has been dubbed "winged tiger." Owls are one of the most important predators of rodents and rabbits; they also prey on skunks, porcupines and other birds.

Owls are beautifully designed for silent night hunting. Their primary feathers have rounded, serrated edges that make little noise as they hunt on the wing. Large, forward-looking eyes surrounded by dish-shaped facial disks increase the amount of light entering the eye for better night vision. But studies have shown hearing is even more important for owls locating prey at night. The bird's ears are asymmetrical, one above the eyeline and one below. The difference in time for sounds to be heard by each ear helps the bird locate the source of the sound. The facial disks also help trap sound and channel it to the ears, much like cupping a hand to your ear.

Great horned owls are early nesters. Beginning in mid-February, they take over the old nest of a hawk, magpie or other bird. While the female sits on the nest, the male roosts in a tree not far away.

When and Where to See Them: Year-round on the plains and in wooded areas and forests throughout the Rockies. They can be found in the mountains up to the edge of the alpine tundra.

EYECATCHERS

The great horned owl is usually found during the day roosting on a tree limb near the trunk, a big cylindrical shape sporting two feathery horns that may blow gently in the breeze. At night you may hear its resonant hooting, a characteristic *hoo oo oo*. Owls may surprise the unwary, flying silently overhead or suddenly swooping past on hushed wings to catch a meal.

Great Horned Owl

Burrowing Owl
A.K.A. Ground owl

Speotyto cunicularia
Family: Owl

A small, stubby-tailed owl about the size and shape of a prairie dog, the burrowing owl has brown plumage with white-flecked back, white neck collar and barred breast. Burrowing owls have large, round, yellow eyes and long legs adapted for life on the ground. The young are tawny with fewer spots and stripes.

Natural History: Burrowing owls arrive in April and May, taking up residence in abandoned prairie dog burrows. The adults coo softly to each other, rubbing necks and bills. They bob and bow comically. When disturbed the young make a noise that sounds like a rattlesnake, in an attempt to scare away predators. When the young emerge from the nest in July, the mound becomes clustered with owls, their feathery bodies pressed together, round, yellow eyes staring intently.

Burrowing owls and prairie dogs are tolerant neighbors, the owls being too small to be a serious threat to their rodent hosts. The owls hunt smaller rodents and insects, though they will eat an occasional young prairie dog, and the dogs in turn sometimes take an unguarded owl egg. Despite their name, burrowing owls don't dig burrows themselves but use abandoned prairie dog holes, relying on their rodent hosts to maintain the burrows.

Biologists fear that this curious owl, so well adapted to life on the treeless plains, is on the decline due to destruction of prairie dog towns for agriculture and development, and poisoning from pesticides used on the insects the owls eat.

When and Where to See Them: Between April and September in grassland prairie dog towns of the United States Rockies. Look for them atop burrow mounds and on nearby fence posts and high points, often in urban areas on open ground where prairie dogs have built a town.

EYECATCHERS

The presence of little brown owls atop the mounds of a prairie dog town may surprise the casual observer, but there's no more certain identifier of burrowing owls.

Burrowing owl standing on edge of burrow

Burrowing owl peeking from burrow

Downy Woodpecker
A.K.A. Downy, little sapsucker

Picoides pubescens
Family: Woodpecker

The smallest woodpeckers in North America, downies have checkered black-and-white wings, a white back and underside, a black crown and broad black-and-white bars across the face. Males have a red spot on the back of the head.

Natural History: *Tap, tap* comes the sound in a quiet wood as the little downy woodpecker probes the bark of a dead tree for insects and grubs. With a relatively short bill that looks less adapted for drilling wood than for eating seeds, the downy is the smallest American woodpecker. A field guide and close scrutiny are necessary to tell downies from hairy woodpeckers, a similar woodpecker that is slightly larger and has a longer bill.

Adapting to life around humans, downies are decorous neighbors, taking up residence in city and suburban trees, checking out feeders and going about their woodpecker chores unperturbed by humans. If you come upon a downy poised on the side of a tree, it will likely not fly off but hop around the tree, peering around the trunk at you from the far side.

Like other woodpeckers, the downy's body is designed to help it drill into trees. The strong, grasping feet, with two toes facing forward and two facing back, let it grip the side of a tree trunk; its sturdy tail braces it as it drums. How do woodpeckers avoid beating their brains out? Their skulls are extra thick and heavy, almost like concrete, to absorb the shock of beating on trees.

In the winter, downies often hang out with chickadees, nuthatches and other birds, coming to birdfeeders to eat suet. Though the little woodpecker's diet is 75 to 85 percent insects, it also eats fruit, seeds and sap, leading to the nickname "little sapsucker."

When and Where to See Them: At backyard feeders, in forests, parklands, orchards and streamside groves throughout the Rockies year-round.

EYECATCHERS

A light tapping sound in an open woodland will clue you to the presence of this little black-and-white woodpecker with a red spot on the back of its head. It has a shorter bill than most woodpeckers.

Downy Woodpecker male

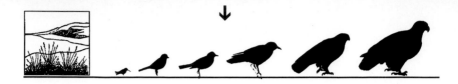

Northern Flicker
A.K.A Wake-up, harrywicket

Colaptes auratus
Family: Woodpecker

The red-shafted flicker is the western subspecies of the northern flicker. The gray-brown back has blackbars; when the bird flies, its white rump flashes and a reddish coloring under wings and tail is visible. Males have a red cheek stripe or "mustache" and both sexes exhibit a black crescent on the upper chest.

Natural History: In a wooded area you hear a rapid, hollow drumming. Then you notice a large bump on the trunk of a tree, but as you approach, the bump flies off with a flash of white and rusty red—a red-shafted flicker.

The flicker is probably the best-known and most common American woodpecker. With its speckled back the flicker is sometimes tough to make out against tree bark. Clinging with strong toes to the trunk of a tree, its cantilevered body and long, sturdy beak positioned to drill, the flicker is built to peck bark. Flickers drill into trees seeking insects for food, but will also forage on the ground, licking up ants with their long, sticky tongues. Woodpecker tongues are amazing tools adapted for the job—twice as long as the bird's head, the tongue retracts into a sheath that wraps around the back and top of the skull. Barbs at the end of the tongue, and sticky saliva, help woodpeckers snare insects inside tree bark.

Flickers nest in holes in trees, fenceposts, telephone poles and the like, excavating the nest hole by pecking. They are important homebuilders for other cavity-nesting birds who, with bills too weak to make their own holes, use those abandoned by woodpeckers.

Both the male and female flicker incubate the eggs and care for the young. When the adults bring food to the nest, they light on the tree, then disappear into the nest cavity. As the babies get older, they learn to expect the parents, poking their heads out of the nest hole and squawking to be fed.

When and Where to See Them: A year-round resident of open woodlands and suburban areas throughout the United States Rockies from the plains into the mountains up to 11,000 feet, flickers migrate to lower elevations in winter. Spring through fall look for them throughout the Rockies into northern Canada.

EYECATCHERS

You may hear the flicker's staccato drumming before you see the bird clinging vertically to the trunk of a tree. You can't miss its white rump and red wings as it flies.

Northern flicker (red-shafted form) peering from nest cavity

Northern flicker males (red-shafted form) in territorial display

Western Kingbird
A.K.A. Arkansas kingbird

Tyrannus verticalis
Family: Tyrant flycatcher

The western kingbird has a gray head and back with sulphur-yellow belly and darker wings and tail. The outer edges of the tail are white.

Natural History: An agile hunter, the kingbird waits on an exposed perch for an insect to fly by, then darts out and snaps it up, returning to the same perch to await the next morsel. In teaching their young to hunt, adults trap and disable insects that they release for the young to catch. Kingbirds like fields, roadsides and brushlands because of the abundance of flying insects.

Kingbirds are named for their pugnacious defense of their territories—they are the "king bird" in their world. They belong to the *Tyrannidae* family of birds, meaning tyrant. Intolerant of trespassers they will dive-bomb and badger hawks and large birds that perch in nearby trees; groups of kingbirds will mob these predators to keep them away from kingbird nests. At times they actually sit on the hawk's neck and peck at its head while the hawk is in flight. The kingbird's shrill bickering call sounds like a tape player on fast forward.

When and Where to See Them: From the first week of May through September sitting on barbed-wire fences and telephone lines and in trees along roadsides and fields from New Mexico into southern British Columbia and Alberta.

> **EYECATCHERS**
>
> These grayish, robin-sized birds are often seen perched on a wire or twig tip. They will mob and drive off magpies and hawks (and humans) in aggressive defense of their nests.

Western Kingbird

Horned Lark

Eremophila alpestris

A.K.A. Snow lark

Family: Lark

This gray-brown bird sports black stripes on the head, black chest collar and "mustache." Small feathery black "horns" on the head can be erected voluntarily or lie flat along the head. The throat is yellow and the breast white.

Natural History: At first glance the horned lark is just another scurrying, nondescript brown bird found commonly on prairies, fields and grasslands. But at the right angle the little feather "horns" on its head become visible, making it look like a tiny "Batman." Jostling with other birds, larks will erect these horns, as if flicking them up at a competitor.

Larks walk or run on the ground rather than hopping like sparrows. As they feed they scurry busily around, incessantly pecking at the ground, displacing each other—one moves over, supplanting a second who moves over and displaces a third. A very common grassland bird, some horned larks nest above timberline on the alpine tundra.

When it comes to impressing females, the courting male lark is no slouch. Not only does he erect his feathery horns and strut about, but his flight performance and song are impressive. Rising up and up in the air with bursts of wingbeats till reaching a great height, his singing still audible high overhead, the male folds his wings and plummets toward the ground.

When and Where to See Them: Throughout the southern Rockies year-round on open prairie and grasslands, moving into mountain parks, open mountain slopes and the alpine tundra up to 14,000 feet in the summer, and breeding throughout the Rockies into northern Canada. Horned larks like dirt fields and gravel patches. In winter they move in large flocks, breaking up into pairs in the early spring.

EYECATCHERS

This lark's black feather "horns" on the head are not always visible, but the distinctive striped pattern on the head and the irregular, tinkling song, often heard even when the bird is far overhead, identify it.

Horned Lark

Barn Swallow

Hirundo rustica
Family: Swallow

Barn swallows are deep, glossy, almost iridescent blue on the back with a buffy orange breast. They have a forked "swallow tail" with white dots on the underside.

Natural History: Barn swallows earned their name from their preference for nesting in barns and under the eaves of buildings. They use mud pellets to build half-cup nests which they "glue" to walls or cliffs. Barn swallows often nest in colonies under bridges and culverts. Their wide mouths are adapted for snapping up insects, with feathery "whiskers" on the sides that act like catcher's mitts to help scoop food into the mouth. Watch for their erratic flight as they swoop and dive after insects, catching them on the wing; you can sometimes hear a clicking sound as their mouths snap shut. On cold days they're often seen milling above water where the warmer air attracts insects. They also skim a drink from the water's surface while on the wing.

Watch for barn swallows at traffic intersections as they dart out to hunt insects during a pause in traffic.

When and Where to See Them: During spring, summer and fall, barn swallows can be seen anywhere on the plains, especially along highways at culverts, lakes and streams, throughout the Rockies.

EYECATCHERS

Look for the barn swallow's deeply forked tail, visible in flight.

Barn Swallow

Adult feeding young in nest

Black-billed Magpie

Pica pica
Family: Crow

The black-billed magpie is a large, striking black-and-white bird with long tail; its black plumage often appears iridescent green. White wing patches flash in flight.

Natural History: Dressed in glossy black tux and tails, the magpie is just wary enough to give the impression of haughtiness. Its habits and adaptability bring it close to humans, but never too close. A gathering of magpies awaiting opportunity is amusing to watch: they mill among the trees or on the ground around a food source, fly up to join each other in the branches, then one after another fly off to another tree. Sociable birds, they nest in loose colonies, their raucous calls distinct among the trees.

Like other members of the crow family, they are opportunists—scavenging, stealing food from other animals, gathering in groups around food. The sight of groups of magpies striding about on the ground around an edible tidbit, then stealing in to grab a bite when the opportunity arises and flying off, is a familiar image. They'll even hop past a sleeping dog to peck at dog bones or steal bits of dog food. Magpies are somewhat wary of humans but frequently live close to people in urban and suburban areas, exploiting trash and available food.

Though adapted for life on the prairie, magpies need trees for nesting. Their large, domed stick nests are easy to see in trees, especially in winter when they appear like a bulge amidst the bare branches. Magpies build a top over their nests, with an entrance on both sides.

In flight their long tails trail behind them like an arrow. Magpies have a raucous call, *cack, cack, cack.*

When and Where to See Them: In open woodlands and rangeland thickets especially near water, magpies are year-round residents from New Mexico into northern Canada at elevations up to about 8,000 feet. A common urban and suburban bird.

EYECATCHERS

This handsome bird's glossy black-and-white plumage, long tail and bold behavior make it impossible to miss.

Black-billed Magpie

American Crow
A.K.A. Common crow

Corvus brachyrhynchos
Family: Crow

The American crow is a large, black bird with a powerful beak; in some light the plumage glimmers an iridescent purple. Crows are smaller and more gregarious than ravens and have a squared-off tail.

Natural History: The crow is part of American folklore, a flimflam bird that tricks other animals, steals goodies and passes gossip. To many people crows are birds with an attitude—sitting in groups on telephone wires like shiftless ne'er-do-wells, projecting an "I know more than you do" attitude.

Crows are canny, intelligent birds, capable of solving problems but also sometimes bothersome. Countless stories tell of crows stealing eggs, flying off with shiny objects, robbing cornfields, even mocking scarecrows by roosting on them. Henry Ward Beecher commented that if men sprouted feathers and wings like birds, very few of them would be smart enough to be crows, while writer David Quammen described them (tongue in cheek) in *Natural Acts* as bored underachievers too intelligent for their station in life.

Sociable birds, crows will hang out together on telephone wires, gathering in large numbers to pass the time of day like gossipy townfolk. They've been observed playing tag or dangling upside down by one foot with wings outstretched as if playing "chicken." As the flock moves into new territory, scouts precede it to check things ou,t and sentinel birds keep watch while the group forages. In evening the flock heads straight back to its nighttime roost "as the crow flies."

Though lacking the melodious voice of a songbird, crows are accomplished mimics; they've been known to make sounds like a child crying, a cackling hen, a crowing rooster, sometimes even cooing like a dove.

When and Where to See Them: Crows are year-round residents of the United States Rockies, found everywhere but in the high mountains. During spring, summer and fall they expand into the Canadian Rockies to breed.

EYECATCHERS

The size, glossy black plumage, brassy manner and familiar *caw* make the crow one of the best-known birds in America.

American Crow in silhouette

Black-capped Chickadee

A.K.A. Black-capped titmouse, eastern chickadee

Parus atricapillus

Family: Titmouse

This little, gray bird has buffy sides, whitish face and underparts and a black throat bib and cap.

Natural History: In a wooded area in spring a bright, clear whistle comes from a tree—*fee-bee*—the first note high, the second several notes lower. If the listener mimics the call the chickadee may answer, perhaps flying closer to perch on a nearby limb and peer down with bright, inquisitive eyes. Sometimes two birds will perform a duet, the second usually answering a tone lower.

Like a little wood sprite, the cheery chickadee is always busy—hopping about, clinging to branches, cocking its head to examine bark for insects or hanging upside down from a twig to peck at a likely tidbit. These amiable birds are gentle and familiar friends, livening the trees year-round with bright activity, in winter visiting feeders in small flocks. While many other birds head south when the weather grows cold, the tiny but tough chickadee stays on to endure winter's hardships, its little body puffed out like a fluffy snowball against the cold.

Though their beaks are small, chickadees often excavate their own nesting holes in soft, rotting stumps or dead trees, lining the cavities with moss, hair, feathers and insect cocoons. Rather than let the excavated chips fall where they may, the adults carry them off and deposit them at a distance, perhaps to hide evidence of their habitation. Both parents share egg incubation duties; if disturbed on the nest they respond with a snakelike hiss designed to scare off intruders.

When and Where to See Them: In deciduous forest, open woodlands and the edge of coniferous forest year-round throughout the Rockies into the Yukon and Alaska.

EYECATCHERS

A sprightly little bird with a black cap, the chickadee utters a two-toned *fee-bee* call and a *chick-a-dee-dee-dee* song, familiar music in open woodlands and amidst city trees.

Black-capped chickadee at entrance to nest cavity

Black-capped Chickadee

American Robin

A.K.A. Robin redbreast

Turdus migratorius

Family: Thrush

The American robin is a gray-brown bird with fox-red breast and white eye ring. The male's breast is a deeper red than the female's and the young have a speckled, orange breast.

Natural History: Everybody knows the robin. It's the first bird of spring, the neighborly, worm-pulling, backyard bird of America. Robins occupy all habitats, from plains to mountain tundra.

One of the first birds to return after winter, the robin symbolizes spring for many people. Males usually arrive first and their friendly song, *cheer-up, cheer-up,* often heard in early morning, heralds the spring blossoms. Some robins overwinter in the Rocky Mountain region, but they become more active and more easily seen when spring arrives.

Females build cuplike nests of mud and grass in trees, frequently in yards and near homes. Broken eggshells of "robin's-egg blue" can often be found on the grass under the nests once the young have hatched. The robin family's proximity to humans makes them great to observe in their everyday life— nest-building, incubating eggs, feeding squawking hatchlings, and finally, the young leaving the nest. The mated pair may lay more eggs and rear a second or even third set of young.

Watching robins hunt is fun; they're as ferocious a predator of worms and insects as a hawk is of mice. Robins hop through the grass, cocking their heads as if listening for insects. Actually, they hunt by sight, not sound, and turn their heads to see better because their eyes are on the sides of their head. When they spot prey in the grass, they grab it with a lightning stab of their long, pointed beaks. Robins also like fruit of any kind, especially the small, plump chokecherries ripening throughout the plains and foothills in late summer and fall.

When and Where to See Them: Late March through the end of summer throughout the Rockies in cities, parks, moist woodlands. Some robins are year-round residents of the southern Rockies.

EYECATCHERS

Look for this red-breasted, hopping, worm-catching bird just about anywhere.

American Robin

Lark Bunting
A.K.A. White-winged blackbird,
prairie finch, prairie bobolink

Calamospiza melanocorys
Family: Finch

This small, black bird with bright white wing patches is usually seen sitting on fenceposts or plant stalks.

Natural History: The flashy black and white lark bunting is a familiar part of the warm weather scene throughout grasslands of the United States Rockies. Along the back roads of plains country in spring and summer they seem to dot every fencepost.

Lark buntings arrive in late April and May on their breeding grounds. The handsome males in their formal black plumage stake out territories and begin to sing. They court the drab gray-brown females with a nuptial song-flight, winging almost straight up in the air then floating down on stiff outstretched wings like a butterfly's, singing all the while.

By the end of summer, with his mating and parental duties completed, the male loses his fancy black-and-white plumage and becomes nearly as drab as the female. The groups of birds that had paired off to breed cluster together again in large flocks visible along country highways. By mid-September they begin their migration south to wintering grounds in the southern United States and Mexico.

When and Where to See Them: From April through mid-September in grasslands and along country roads throughout the United States Rockies into southern Canada. They occur occasionally in mountain parks up to 8,000 feet.

EYECATCHERS

Rigged out in formal black with striking white wing patches, the male lark bunting in breeding plumage is unmistakable on open grasslands.

Lark Bunting

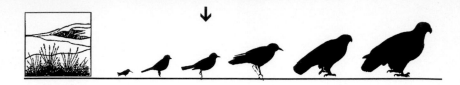

Western Meadowlark
A.K.A. Yellow lark

Sturnella neglecta
Family: Troupial

A robin-sized bird with mottled gray-brown back, the western meadowlark displays a bright yellow breast and black V chest collar.

Natural History: Bobbing on top of a weed stalk along roadsides or in fields, or sitting on a fencepost, head tossed back, bill open and singing cheerfully, the meadowlark is surely the bird of the prairie. Its wonderful, melodic song seems to tumble joyfully across the grasslands of the west. To some pioneers the yellow lark seemed to say *Methodist prea-cher* and *gee whiz whillikers.*

Images of the meadowlark are a familiar part of the prairie landscape—the bird sitting atop a weedstalk, bill open in a wide V as it sings, or flying with a series of choppy wingbeats followed by a short glide, revealing white tail patches.

When courting, the male fans its tail and wings, then jumps into the air with its bill pointed skyward, displaying its bright yellow breast and black chest V.

Meadowlarks build well-hidden ground nests of dried grass and weeds, often with tunnels through the grass. When the female is sitting on the eggs she may not flush until practically stepped on.

When and Where to See Them: Prairies, meadows and open areas at low elevations year-round through the southern Rockies, breeding into Wyoming and Alberta. They may be found in summer in mountain parks up to about 7,000 feet.

EYECATCHERS

The wonderfully melodious *chirtly-chir* call of the meadowlark is the song of the prairie and a sure clue to this bird of the plains. You'll see its bright yellow breast with the black V on the chest and the white flash of the outer tail feathers when the bird flies.

Western Meadowlark

Western meadowlark singing

Bullock's Oriole

A.K.A. Hammock bird

Icterus bullockii

Family: Troupial

This bright orange perching bird has a black head, wings and throat and white wing patches. The female is orange-yellow above with lighter belly and throat.

Natural History: Whether the eastern Baltimore oriole and the western Bullock's oriole are the same species has been the subject of much debate. First they were considered separate, then they were combined as one species, the northern oriole. Now they are once again defined as two separate species. Not only do these two orioles look a little different, one has its own baseball team. Once separated by the Great Plains, the two species now interbreed freely, their ranges brought together by the planting of trees across the Midwest.

The oriole clues us to its presence in many ways. In spring and summer the flashy males zip like orange-and-black comets among the branches of trees and shrubs. Their musical call, a loud series of whistles and chatters, comes from the tops of the trees where they sit and survey their territory. After mating, the drab females weave their nests in less than a week from long grasses and fibers cinched up to form a bag.

The curious, pouch-like nests hang from tree branches like socks left to dry, persisting forlornly into winter long after the birds have migrated south. If the nest is still there in the spring, the birds won't re-use it, but build a brand-new one, sometimes on the same branch next to the old nest. Males sometimes help with the nest-building and incubating, and feed the female when she is on the nest.

Orioles feed on insects, fruit and nectar and will occasionally come to a hummingbird feeder.

When and Where to See Them: In open woodlands, cottonwood groves and suburban shade trees throughout the United States Rockies into southern Canada. Watch for them from May through late August.

EYECATCHERS

Watch for a flash of bright orange as this perching bird darts among the trees, issuing a loud, melodious song from the tops of trees.

Bullock's Oriole

Bullock's Oriole

House Finch

Carpodacus mexicanus

A.K.A. Rose-breasted finch, burrion, crimson-fronted finch

Family: Finch

A brownish gray, sparrowlike bird, the male has a bright red cap, throat and rump. The female is brown with a lighter, streaked underside.

Natural History: House finches are well named because they flock to bird-feeders all winter and are probably one of the most common city birds. Unlike other species hurt by human encroachment, the house finch flourishes around people, taking advantage of city trees, shrubs and landscaping for nesting, and willingly coming to feed on what humans have to offer. In spring the finch's cheery song announces the awakening season, especially in the city.

Since house finches are so common near homes, keep an eye out in spring for the male's courtship of the female. He starts by following her, singing and fluttering his wings. Then he erects the feathers on his head like a little crest, droops his wings, raises his tail and hops about her, singing all the while. If she's sufficiently impressed, they mate. Leave out bits of cotton for the female to use in nestbuilding; you may be rewarded with a house finch nest near your home.

After rearing one set of young, the female may have as many as two more families in the season, sometimes building a new nest, other times reusing the old.

When and Where to See Them: Year-round in low elevation, often semi-arid woodlands , into foothills through the United States Rockies into southern British Columbia. Very common in urban areas.

EYECATCHERS

An otherwise nondescript brown bird, the male displays a distinctive red head and throat. House finches are one of the most common feeder birds.

House Finch male

House Finch female

Birds of the Wetlands

Western Grebe
American White Pelican
Double-crested Cormorant
Great Blue Heron
Black-crowned Night Heron
Snow Goose
Canada Goose
Wood Duck
Mallard
Northern Pintail
Blue-winged Teal
Northern Shoveler
Redhead
Osprey
Bald Eagle
Northern Harrier
American Coot
Sandhill Crane
Killdeer
American Avocet
Spotted Sandpiper
Common Snipe
Ring-billed Gull
Belted Kingfisher
Red-winged Blackbird
Yellow-headed Blackbird
Common Yellowthroat

Western Grebe

Aechmophorus occidentalis
Family: Grebe

The western grebe is a long-necked waterbird with two-toned plumage—black mask on the top of the head and around the eye, black down the back of the neck, white on the throat and underside of the neck.

Natural History: Once you've seen the eerily graceful spring courtship dance of the western grebe you'll never forget this handsome bird. The dance begins with a male and female following each other, bobbing their heads and giving a scratchy *kree-eek* call. Then they swim straight toward each other, intertwining necks and pirouetting slowly in a circle. Swimming side by side like mirror images, the two posture with their necks and heads. Finally they rise up on the water and run across the surface together in a flurry of splashing.

Neither duck nor goose, the grebe is a waterbird with lobed rather than webbed feet. Unlike the flat bill of ducks, grebes have a pointed bill for plucking small fish and other prey from the water. The grebe's legs are set at the back of its body, a position that facilitates diving but hinders the bird's ability to walk. Grebes are rarely seen on land or flying, though they are migratory. Truly at home on the water, grebes build floating nests anchored to reeds and vegetation in shallow water. Once hatched the fledglings hitch a ride on their parents' backs, holding on with their bills when the adults dive.

When and Where to See Them: On lower elevation lakes and reservoirs from New Mexico through Montana from April to September. Courtship occurs in late April and early May.

EYECATCHERS

The striking color contrast of black and white and the low profile in the water are characteristic. The grebe often looks like a bodyless neck jutting from the water.

Western Grebe

American White Pelican   *Pelecanus erythrorhynchos*
Family: Pelican

A great, white waterbird with black wingtips, the American white pelican has a curving neck and a long, orange bill with a skin pouch below. Arguably the largest bird in North America, its wingspan spreads up to nine and a half feet.

Natural History: "A wonderful bird is the pelican, / His bill will hold more than his belican." Immortalized by Dixon L. Merritt, the pelican is indeed a wonderful bird, one dear to the heart of any wildlife watcher. Ungainly and comical in appearance, pelicans are nevertheless powerful fliers and swimmers, floating on the water's surface like flotillas of white-sailed ships, all facing the same direction. Pelicans utilize cooperative group hunting techniques, some of the birds "herding" fish toward other pelicans or into shallow water where they are more easily gobbled up. White pelicans float on the water's surface, using their wonderful pouched bills like nets to dip fish from the water; unlike brown pelicans, they don't dive below the surface after food.

Pelicans fly at great heights, like white streamers in a blue sky, the large flocks flashing in and out of the clouds. Descending like a winged air force, they circle in to land gracefully on the water's surface, sometimes flying so low overhead the individual feathers of their black wingtips are discernible. Like vacationers at the beach, a group of pelicans may sit on a patch of shore sunning themselves, all facing in the same direction with their bills in the air.

In spring during breeding season the adults develop a noticeable bump, called a breeding board, plate or fin, on the top of their bills. Unfortunately breeding colonies have declined severely. This fascinating bird may be vanishing due to pesticide poisoning, shooting and human harassment; human visitors who come too close to nests often scare away the brooding adults, leaving the helpless nestlings exposed to predators and the midday sun.

When and Where to See Them: In spring and fall migration on larger ponds and lakes through the United States Rockies and into the prairies of Canada. Breeding is highly localized throughout this range.

EYECATCHERS

The pelican's great size and startling whiteness, its long, pouched, yellow bill and its habit of flying and swimming in formation make it unmistakable.

American white pelicans fishing together

Pelicans herding fish by beating the water with their wings

Double-crested Cormorant

A.K.A. Shag, taunton turkey

Phalacrocorax auritus

Family: Cormorant

The cormorant is a large, black waterbird with a hooked bill and a patch of bare yellow skin under the bill. Breeding adults have two feathery "crests" on the head.

Natural History: Because the cormorant's legs attach at the very end of its body, rather than underneath like a duck's, it walks awkwardly on land. Like a loon, the cormorant has a low profile in the water, its neck curved snakelike and its head tipped slightly up, "nose-in-the-air."

Cormorants are superb fishers, diving underwater and chasing down their prey. Using their feet as paddles to propel themselves forward they flap their wings to "fly" underwater. Their hooked bills help them hang onto slippery fish. Cormorants may dive as deep as twenty-five feet, staying underwater up to seventy seconds.

Rocks and logs around lakes are good places to spot resting cormorants as they sit in the sun with their wings spread-eagled to dry. Why must they dry their wings, while the plumage of ducks and geese is waterproof? Scientists have learned that waterproof plumage is due more to the structure of the feathers than to waterproof oils. This waterproof structure also makes the feathers buoyant. Cormorant feather structure reduces buoyancy and helps them dive and pursue fish underwater. The down side of this means their feathers don't repel water very well, and after a swim the cormorant must dry its wings in the sun. Luckily the cormorant has a waterproof inner layer of feathers near the body; its coat may get wet but inside it stays dry and warm.

Cormorants are sociable birds; if you see one you're likely to find a whole colony. They build basket-shaped nests of sticks in the upper branches of trees and shrubs around lakes and reservoirs.

Because of their size and long necks cormorants often fool people, who think they are Canada geese. But while geese honk noisily, cormorants are more discreet and maintain their silence. Watch how their pattern of flying differs from a goose—flap, flap, cruise—instead of the goose's steady wingbeats.

When and Where to See Them: From April through early November on larger inland lakes and plains reservoirs from the central Rockies into Canada. Occasional sightings the rest of the year.

EYECATCHERS

In flight the cormorant looks like a black goose, but unlike the goose it flies in silence, propelled by irregular wingbeats. Perching, the cormorant is unmistakable with its curving neck and upright pose, occasionally holding its wings out to dry. On the water the cormorant has such a low profile it may often look like a periscope—just a long neck sticking up out of the water, its hooked bill tipped slightly up.

Double-crested Cormorant

Double-crested cormorants drying their feathers

Great Blue Heron

A.K.A. Blue crane, great blue

Ardea herodias
Family: Heron

A large, gray-blue wading bird, the great blue heron stands up to four feet tall, with very long neck, long stilt legs and spear-like bill. Its head is whitish, trailing a plume of blue or black feathers. Breeding adults have feathery plumes on the chest.

Natural History: The great blue heron is not only a common denizen of wetland areas, but perhaps the most impressive. Circling above a pond or marsh on large wings, great blue herons seem like incredible flying reptiles from another age, slowly surveying a primordial swamp.

Great blues build large stick nests in the upper reaches of cottonwoods, circling in to settle in the treetops in an awkward folding of long legs, large wings and snakelike neck. The big, gawky birds roost among the bare branches of cottonwoods, their nests like snagged clumps in the branches, silhouetted against the sky. The heronries are a riot of bird activity and noise, the roar of great wings, the cackles of nestlings and the croaking calls of the adults. The birds return year after year to the same heronry, staying true even when the trees that hold their nests die and become unstable, threatening entire nesting colonies.

If you've ever waded in a shallow pond you can appreciate the hunting skill of a great blue heron. Lifting a foot above the water's surface, then setting it down oh-so-softly, the heron moves stealthily, disturbing the water only slightly. It may stand motionless, eyeballing fish, frogs and aquatic invertebrates with its telescopic vision before plucking them lightning fast from the water with its rapier bill.

When and Where to See Them: Mid-March through October on marsh-lined lakes, streams, canals and wetlands of the plains and mountain valleys of the southern, central and northern Rockies through southern Alaska, with some birds resident in the more southern range.

EYECATCHERS

Watch for this large blue bird circling a stream or pond on huge wings, or wading ever so cautiously in shallow water. Often mistaken for cranes, herons fly with their long necks folded in an S so they appear neckless, rather than extended like a crane.

Great blue heron on dead limb of a cottonwood tree

Great blue heron in flight

Black-crowned Night Heron

Nycticorax nycticorax
Family: Heron

A.K.A. Quawk, buttermunk, bittrun, bull bittrun, plunket, wagin, grosbec

This medium-sized heron has a glossy black back and crown, gray wings and tail and a white face and underparts. Its legs and feet are yellow and its eyes red. It has a short neck, thick bill and two or three long, white plumes trailing from the head.

Natural History: Aptly named, the black-crowned night heron is a creature of the night. Though it may be visible roosting in trees at the edge of a marsh during the day—sitting hunched like a sullen teenager on spraddled stick legs—the night heron stirs to activity at dusk, suddenly leaving its daytime roost and flying over the marsh in the gathering dark like a great bat. Its harsh cry is one of the night sounds of the marsh.

Night herons nest in colonial heronries near other waterbirds, their large stick nests set like baskets in the branches of waterside cottonwoods and willows. The activity in the heronry is like that of a busy, noisy apartment house—cormorants and great blue herons in the upper branches of cottonwoods, the smaller night herons in the lower branches and low willows, all of them coming in, taking off, feeding their garrulous young, and keeping up a constant din. After spending a night near a heronry, ornithologist Edward Howe Forbush reported, "A nervous person might have imagined that the souls of the condemned had been thrown into purgatory, and were bemoaning their fate . . . cat-calls, infant screams, shrieks, yells and croaks swelled the chorus, all intermingled with the beating of heavy wings."

These wading birds step carefully through the mud flats and shallow water, watching for fish and other aquatic animals. The young become adept at climbing from the nest into the treetops even before they can fly, using feet, bill and wings to scramble up into the higher branches

When and Where to See Them: Late March through October in marshy areas along lower elevation streams and lakes throughout the United States Rockies into central Alberta.

EYECATCHERS

You'll know the night heron when you see it slouching in a marshland tree, its shoulders hunched and its chin sunk on its breast. Or you may just hear its harsh *quok* call as it flies over at dusk, a seemingly neckless, tailless bird with pointed bill.

Black-crowned Night Heron

Snow Goose
A.K.A. Blue goose (dark phase)

Chen caerulescens
Family: Duck

This handsome wild goose is smaller than a domestic goose and has two strikingly different color phases. The more common white phase is pure white with black wingtips. Its bill and feet are pink. The blue phase has a dark grayish blue body with white neck and head.

Natural History: With high-pitched calls, a trailing flock of large, white birds passes high overhead—the snow geese. These wild geese, snowy white in color, are truly creatures of the far north. Each year they make the annual migration thousands of miles from wintering grounds as far south as northern Mexico to nest on the barren tundra of the Arctic. On their way north the geese gather at staging areas at prairie potholes and marshes, fattening for the long journey. Snow geese are grazers, eating grasses, sedges, berries, and waste grain in fields.

The two color phases of snow goose were long thought to be separate species. In 1929 a nesting area of "blue geese" was found near Hudson Bay. Observation of the two types of geese revealed that they interbreed, producing an intermediate phase, and the two were reclassified as one species.

Snow geese gather in colonies, sometimes tens of thousands of individuals. Because of the short breeding season on the tundra, snow geese lay only one clutch of eggs. If spring is late, they may not nest at all.

When and Where to See Them: Unless you venture out on the Arctic tundra of far northern Canada in summer, you'll need to watch for snow geese along the flyway east of the Rockies in early spring and fall, or visit wintering grounds in New Mexico and northern Mexico. Thousands of snow geese winter at the Bosque del Apache National Wildlife Refuge south of Albuquerque, New Mexico.

EYECATCHERS

The snow goose is snowy white with black wingtips. Watch for large flocks of white geese flying overhead in spring or fall or gathering in great numbers at marshland staging areas.

Snow Goose

Canada Goose
A.K.A. Honker

Branta canadensis
Family: Duck

This large, wild goose has grayish-brown plumage, a striking long, black neck and black head with white chinstrap and cheek patches.

Natural History: Who isn't compelled to look up when a flight of Canada geese wings overhead in autumn, their honking echoing the voice of wildness? We don't know why they fly in V-shaped formations, but the restless, determined flock trailing off to the horizon, their honking audible even after they've disappeared, is a powerful image of autumn.

Canada geese mate for life, returning over many seasons to nest at the same site. If one mate is killed or dies, the other may remain unpaired for a season or more. Though geese originally migrated south from the central Rockies in winter, the construction of so many reservoirs along the Front Range of the Rockies has caused many geese to stay year-round.

Geese nest along the water's edge, the female braving early spring snowstorms to incubate her eggs. A few days after hatching, the young follow the parents to water and the family goes for a swim, the cluster of fuzzy, black-and-yellow goslings trailing their regal-looking parents like a string of beads.

Geese are grazers and often cause problems on golf courses, city parks and lawns when groups of them gather to feed, cropping the grass to bare earth and leaving accumulations of droppings.

While a flock is grazing, "sentinels" keep watch, honking an alarm call when danger approaches. On water the group will drift out of harm's way. When they court or squabble, geese lower their heads, extend their long necks and hiss at each other.

When and Where to See Them: Wherever there's open water and grass, geese are likely to gather—ponds, reservoirs, golf courses, parks, even bits of landscaping and water around office buildings. Visible spring, summer and fall throughout the Rockies, many geese remain year-round in southern breeding grounds.

EYECATCHERS

The honking of the wild geese winging overhead in great, trailing Vs may be your first clue to these birds' presence. Even at a distance their large size, long, black necks with white chin and cheeks are unmistakable.

Canada Goose

Canada goose nesting

Wood Duck

A.K.A. **Summer duck, tree duck, acorn duck**

Aix sponsa

Family: Duck

Flashy and brightly colored, the male wood duck has an iridescent green-and-purple head marked with white stripes and a dramatic swept-back feather crest. The female is grayish brown with a small crest, white neck and white spot around the eye.

Natural History: A duck that climbs trees? Sounds odd, but the wood duck nests in trees, choosing a tree cavity often fairly high above ground. One nest was recorded at a height of sixty-five feet, but about thirty feet is more typical. The ducks don't really climb trees but fly into the branches. Still, it's a bizarre sight to see ducks perching in a tree.

The parents line the nest with wood chips and downy feathers. Soon after the eggs hatch, the mother calls to the ducklings, and they jump out of the nest hole, sometimes tumbling to the ground with a thump, and follow her to water. The young have very sharp claws and a hook on the end of their bills to help them climb up out of the nest hole. Heavy hunting, timber-cutting and general habitat loss brought wood ducks nearly to extinction by the early part of the twentieth century. Artificial nest boxes have helped increase populations.

Wood ducks are truly the most beautiful of waterfowl, the male resplendent in gleaming, metallic plumage of green, blue, purple and white, his face painted, his head trailing a regal crest. Courtship begins in the fall, with groups of wood ducks gliding elegantly on streams and small pools, both males and females performing—flashing wings, tails and head crests; coyly bobbing their heads or dipping their bills in the water; often calling softly. Once mates are chosen, the pair stays together and away from other wood ducks that are still performing in groups. If separated the mated pair gives a little greeting on being reunited, flicking their bills rapidly in the air.

On the water wood ducks seem to bob higher than other ducks and appear almost neckless.

When and Where to See Them: In spring, summer and early fall on tree-lined lakes, streams and rivers or open woodlands along water, with scattered breeding throughout the central Rockies into southern British Columbia.

EYECATCHERS

The wood duck's flashy coloration and sweeping, debonair head crest make it impossible to confuse with other ducks. You may hear its *weep, weep, weep* cry without ever seeing it fly off through the trees.

Wood Duck male

Wood Duck female

Mallard
A.K.A. Greenhead, curlytail

Anas platyrhynchos
Family: Duck

A very familiar large, gray duck, the male mallard has a shiny, emerald-green head with a white neck ring. The female is a nondescript brown. Both have purplish blue wing patches edged in white.

Natural History: The common mallard is the bird that most comes to mind when we think of a wild duck. Seen everywhere, this mild-mannered duck with the beautiful emerald head has become a familiar neighbor on ponds, streams, parks and golf courses. Its comical habit of tipping "bottoms up" when feeding creates an amusing scene at busy ponds that become dotted with duck tails pointing toward the sky.

The mallard drake's courtship display is familiar, though we may not know that's what we've seen. He shakes his head and his tail, often rising with his breast partway out of the water. He also shows himself off by raising his wingtips, tail and head in a "head-up, tail-up" display. In turn the female may do an "inciting display" to get males to attack other males, perhaps so she can judge their suitability as mates. This can include swimming toward a group of males with neck outstretched and head just above the water, or, when a strange male approaches, swimming after her prospective mate, quacking and flicking her head sideways.

Mallard mating can be a disturbing sight to the unprepared. Pursuing the hapless female, on the shore and in the water, the mallard drake clambers up on her back, pecking at her head and forcing it underwater during mating.

Though the mated pair are monogamous during the breeding season, the drake deserts the hen soon after she lays the eggs, leaving her to rear the young while he joins bands of other males. They will each choose different mates the next season.

The downy mallard hatchlings leave the nest within about twenty-four hours of hatching and follow their mother to water. They swim behind her like a troop of fuzzy balls, trailing in and out of reeds and pond vegetation.

When and Where to See Them: On the plains and in mountain valleys on open water, puddles, streams or wherever there's a bit of standing water, throughout the Rockies from spring through fall. Many resident birds inhabit the southern and central Rockies.

EYECATCHERS
The mallard drake's green head is as familiar and distinguishing as Lincoln's stovepipe hat.

Mallard male

Mallard female

Northern Pintail

A.K.A. Sprig tail, pheasant duck, gray duck, picket-tail, sea wigeon

Anas acuta
Family: Duck

This handsome bronze-brown duck reveals a white stripe on the side of the head extending down the underside of the neck. The head is a solid brown and the body a mottled gray-brown. A few long, black feathers protrude from the tail. The female is a drab mottled brown.

Natural History: The pintail is a common duck, bobbing gracefully on ponds and lakes with its arrow tail held high. The pintail pair "meet" and bond during winter; the male then follows the female to her nesting ground. A fickle lover, he abandons her soon after the eggs are laid and seeks out other females to mate with.

Pintails often make their nests in relatively exposed areas far from water, concealing them in grass and stubble. The disturbed hen may startle hikers in a field or meadow by starting up suddenly from underfoot, flapping and honking in distress. Like a killdeer, the female pintail will feign injury to draw intruders away from her nest.

Pintails are opportunists, appearing on field puddles and temporary bodies of water to forage while the chance exists, then moving on when those dry up. They seem particularly sociable with mallards and the two species are often seen together. They even occasionally interbreed.

Like mallards, pintails are dabbling ducks—they feed in the mud at the pond bottom—and their populations have suffered heavily from lead shot poisoning. Because waste shot sinks to the muddy bottom, pintails ingest great amounts of lead and gradually die from lead poisoning. An estimated 1.5 to 3 million waterfowl die annually from lead poisoning.

When and Where to See Them: March through October on marshes and open water throughout the Rockies, with many living year-round in the southern Rockies.

EYECATCHERS

This duck's "pin tail"—long, pointed feathers extending up at an angle—and its snowy white throat contrasting to otherwise brown plumage make it stand out easily among other ducks.

Female (left) and male (right) northern pintail

Male showing water droplets after diving

Blue-winged Teal
A.K.A. Blue-wing, summer teal

Anas discors
Family: Duck

This mottled, brownish gray duck has a bold white crescent behind its bill, and a black tail. Watch for powder-blue wing patches when it flies. The female is a nondescript brown.

Natural History: Already paired up when they arrive in their breeding grounds in the spring, the male blue-winged teal still courts his female. Like mallards, blue-winged teal are dabbling or "puddle" ducks (their courtship displays are very similar to mallards). Unlike mallards they don't bob bottoms-up when feeding, but prefer to skim the water with their flat bills or reach below the surface in the shallows to feed on the pond bottom.

Blue-wings fly in compact, tight-turning flocks, rushing back and forth above a prospective site until satisfied it is a safe spot to land, then lighting suddenly on the water as a group. The breeding range and habitat of the blue-winged teal overlap with the cinnamon teal, and the two ducks occasionally interbreed. However, the blue-wings seem less tolerant of cold than other ducks and are the last to arrive in spring and the first to move south again in fall. They build nests of grass and stalks on dry ground near water, usually well concealed under arching vegetation.

When and Where to See Them: April through October on lakes, marshes and open water from prairies to foothills throughout the Rockies.

EYECATCHERS

When this trim little duck flies, its bright blue wing patch flashes like a patch of sky. The bright white crescent behind its bill is another identifier.

Male blue-winged teal preening while female feeds

Male blue-winged teal preening

Northern Shoveler
A.K.A. Spoonbill, broadbill

Anas clypeata
Family: Duck

A boldly colored, medium-sized dabbling duck with a long, spoon-shaped bill, the male has a glossy green head and neck, white breast and flank, rusty-red sides with gray wings. As with most ducks the female is an unremarkable brown.

Natural History: Looking like a bulbous-nosed cartoon character, the shoveler goes through life with a comical spoon-shaped bill that seems about to catch in the water and trip it up. Of course nature wasn't playing a trick on this duck by giving it such a bill. Beautifully designed for dabbling in the water, the shoveler's bill scoops mud from the pond bottom, sifting out bits of food though comb-like "teeth" along the edge of the bill. It may skim the water's surface straining out edible plants and animals. The shoveler's bill is so much better developed than those of other ducks that it can catch minute edibles their bills can't. Shovelers will sometimes feed in a tight group, swimming slowly in a circle, straining the material stirred up in the water by their feet.

Despite their ungainly appearance, shovelers are good fliers and when startled rise up suddenly from the water and dart off in quick, erratic flight. Once calmed they often settle back to the spot from which they were flushed. Shovelers build their nests in concealed depressions on high, dry land sometimes quite far from water.

When and Where to See Them: Mid-April through mid-October on ponds and shallow, open water throughout the Rockies.

EYECATCHERS

The shoveler's comical spoon-shaped bill sets it apart in any crowd. The bold blocks of color—green head, white breast and reddish sides—are easily seen even at a distance.

Northern Shovelers, male (left) and female (right)

Redhead
A.K.A. Red-headed raft duck

Aythya americana
Family: Duck

The male redhead has a large, round chestnut-red head, gray body and black chest and tail. The bill is blue with a black tip. As with most ducks the female is an unremarkable brown.

Natural History: Unlike mallards, teal and pintail, which are dabblers, the redhead is a diving duck that ventures below the water's surface to feed on submerged vegetation, insects, snails, tadpoles and crustaceans. To help propel itself it has large feet situated toward the back of its body.

Redheads build nests of reeds anchored to the emergent vegetation in shallow water. They incubate their own eggs but are also nest parasites, often laying their eggs in other birds' nests. They may parasitize the nest of another redhead, or choose a totally different species of duck, most frequently mallards. (One researcher observed thirteen different redhead hens laying eggs in the same mallard nest!) Or they may lay part of a clutch in someone else's nest, while keeping a few to sit on themselves.

The redhead is similar to the canvasback, a larger duck with the same coloration but a longer, black bill and sloping rather than rounded forehead.

When and Where to See Them: Look for redheads in spring, summer and early fall in marshlands with open water and on vegetation-lined ponds and lakes, breeding through the central Rockies into British Columbia and southern Alberta.

EYECATCHERS

The redhead is painted in blocks of color—black chest and tail, grayish white middle, and round red head with blue bill.

Redhead with water droplets after diving

Redhead flapping its wings

Osprey
A.K.A. Fish eagle, fish hawk

Pandion haliaetus
Family: Hawk

This large hawk with charcoal back and wings flashes white undersides as it flies overhead. The white head has a crest of trailing feathers and a horizontal black stripe through the eye. In flight black wrist patches are evident.

Natural History: A large raptor flies slowly above the surface of a lake, peering down into the water. Suddenly it swoops down, slashing the surface with its talons. Flapping its wings with strong strokes to break free of the water's drag, the osprey rises into the air, a fish gripped firmly in its talons.

Watching an osprey hunt is a thrill—the dramatic feetfirst dive, the slash of talons as it snags an unsuspecting fish from the water. In flight ospreys always carry fish headfirst, probably to reduce wind resistance. Unlike bald eagles, which eat fish, mammals, carrion and a variety of food, ospreys feed only on fish.

The osprey is a vocal bird, uttering a variety of chirps and squeals. Its most frequent call is a high pitched whistle.

Though perhaps not at ease around humans, ospreys have learned to tolerate human activity and will build their large stick nests on floating buoys, utility poles and human-made nest towers, sometimes in parks and near homes if there is open water and a good food source nearby. If undisturbed they will return to the same nest year after year.

Unfortunately, osprey populations suffered greatly in recent decades from shooting, habitat loss and DDT poisoning and have only begun to recover after careful conservation efforts including building of artificial nest platforms.

When and Where to See Them: In spring and fall, migrant osprey visit lower elevation reservoirs and waterways of the southern and central Rockies. They nest from the central through the northern Rockies, wintering from the southern United States south.

EYECATCHERS

Look for a large hawklike bird, smaller than an eagle, hunting low over the surface of the water. The black eyestripe on the white head is distinctive.

Osprey

Osprey with wings extended

Bald Eagle
**A.K.A. White-headed eagle,
American eagle, Washington eagle**

Haliaeetus leucocephalus
Family: Hawk

A very large bird of prey, the adult bald eagle has brown plumage with unmistakable snowy white head and tail, yellow beak, legs and feet. Immature birds lack the white head and have mottled white markings on the tail and underparts.

Natural History: The first sight of a bald eagle touches a chord inside the viewer, evoking a sense of something wild and untamable, something beyond man's harnessing. Perhaps more than any other bird, the eagle represents wildness —its size, strength and power make it a natural symbol of our nation.

The large shapes of eagles roosting in trees along a waterway or lake are sometimes surprising. With their piercing gaze, hooked beaks and proud heads they seem like masters surveying their world.

Eagle courtship is an incredible sight, much of it taking place on the wing as the two birds soar and dive together, sometimes linking talons and tumbling hundreds of feet through the air locked together. The eagle pair mates for life, building large stick nests in the upper branches of trees near water. The pair adds to the nest each year; one nest used for thirty-four years measured eight feet across, twelve feet deep, and weighed two tons. Nests like this eventually kill the supporting tree.

Because the bald eagle plucks fish from the water, its legs are unfeathered to reduce drag. These fish-eaters also prey on waterfowl and mammals. Balds are great pirates, harassing and chasing ospreys and other birds of prey, forcing them to drop their meal. This larcenous habit caused Benjamin Franklin to consider the bald eagle "of bad moral character and not fit to become America's national bird." Eagles also eat a great deal of carrion. Their call is a weak, chattering sound surprising for such a magnificent animal.

Shamefully, bald eagle numbers fell drastically in the twentieth century from hunting, habitat loss, and DDT poisoning. Fortunately, recovery efforts have succeeded. In 1995, the bald eagle was downlisted from an endangered to a threatened species in most of the United States.

When and Where to See Them: Along lakes, rivers and open water, bald eagles winter in the southern and central Rockies, moving in spring into the northern Rockies to breed. Some breeding birds of the southern and central Rockies are non-migratory.

EYECATCHERS
This magnificent eagle is unmistakable with its fine, white head and great size. Whether roosting in a tree or wheeling in the air while on the hunt, eagles have a commanding presence.

Bald Eagle

Northern Harrier
A.K.A. Marsh hawk, hen harrier

Circus cyaneus
Family: Hawk

The northern harrier is a slender hawk with long tail and wings. The male is pearl gray with black wingtips; the larger female is brown with a streaked underside. Immature birds are cinnamon colored underneath. All have a white rump band at the base of the tail and a dish-shaped ruff of feathers forming the owl-like face.

Natural History: While many hawks sit atop poles waiting for their next meal to come by, harriers actively hunt for their food, systematically quartering fields or marshes and "harrying" their prey. Equipped like an owl with a sound-gathering ruff of feathers around the head, harriers fly close to the ground, looking for motion and listening for the squeak of mice and small animals in the grass below. They also feed on small birds they flush from the reeds and grasses.

In spring, males court females by performing spectacular U-shaped patterns in the air, flying straight up, then folding their wings and plummeting downward into a loop, only to climb straight up into another one. The two exchange food talon to talon in mid-air, or drop food for the other to catch on the wing. They nest in wetlands, building a grassy nest on the ground.

Harriers are usually silent, sometimes making a weak, nasal whistle, but can loudly defend their nest sites, diving at people who come too close. At this time the call is a loud, chattering *yip*.

When and Where to See Them: In late fall, winter and early spring hunting over old fields, grasslands and marshes. They maintain a lower profile and are harder to see the rest of the year. If they're seen in the summer, they're probably nesting somewhere closeby. Harriers breed from the central Rockies into northern Canada and Alaska, living year-round in the southern Rockies.

> **EYECATCHERS**
>
> Watch for a large, white rump band visible in flight. Also distinctive is the slow, buoyant, teetering flight just a few feet above the ground, with wings tipped up at a V rather than held flat.

Northern harrier female photographed at the Rocky Mountain Raptor Program, Colorado State University—a rehabilitation center for injured raptors in Fort Collins, Colorado. This bird is used in educational programs.

Northern harrier hunting

American Coot
A.K.A. Mudhen, mud duck, whitebill, sea crow, blue peter, blue marsh hen, crow duck, pond hen, pond crow

Fulica americana
Family: Rail

A black waterbird that looks like a duck, but isn't, the coot has a white, chickenlike bill rather than a duck bill, and a small head. It has large, white spots on the covert feathers under its tail.

Natural History: Few waterbirds are as amusing to watch as the coot, which seems to be found everywhere there's open water. Gabbling, cackling, chasing each other around the water, the squabbling coot has well earned the nickname "mudhen." One coot challenges another, extending its neck menacingly on the surface of the water as it swims toward its neighbor. Suddenly it chases the other bird across the water in a flurry of splashing and fluttering wings. After such an encounter the coots tip up their tails to expose the white spots beneath, like two big eyes staring at the opponent.

The coot pushes its head back and forth as it swims as if it needs this pump-handle motion to power its paddling.

Coots are prolific breeders, building bulky platform nests of reeds among the tules and cattails and averaging ten to twelve eggs in a single clutch. The young are red the first few days after hatching. Once out of the nest they may hitch a ride on the backs of their swimming parents, hanging on tenaciously with their bills when the adults dive.

When and Where to See Them: On open water and in marshy areas to mid-elevation mountains throughout the Rockies from March through October. Many coots live year-round in the more temperate areas of their range.

EYECATCHERS

The coot's behavior as much as its white bill identifies it. The coot pokes its head back and forth as it swims, and squabbles frequently with other coots, squawking and gabbling like a chicken.

American Coot

Sandhill Crane

Grus canadensis

A.K.A. Brown crane, blue crane, turkey crane

Family: Crane

The sandhill crane stands up to four feet tall—a big, gray bird with a naked red forehead, long stick legs and a long neck. The wings have black tips.

Natural History: The annual migration of the sandhill cranes through the Rockies recreates a scene from the past, when great gatherings of wildlife were common in North America. The cranes pause to feed in Colorado's San Luis Valley on their spring migration from New Mexico to nesting grounds in northwest Colorado, Wyoming, Idaho and Montana. They gather in great numbers, roosting at night in marshy bottomlands and moving out into the grainfields during the day to feed on waste grain. Each spring 18,000 to 20,000 greater sandhill cranes pass through the valley. Even larger numbers of lesser sandhill cranes, up to half a million, pass through central Nebraska each spring on their way to Arctic nesting grounds.

In the San Luis Valley the cranes perform an eerily elegant courtship dance in preparation for breeding. Across the fields comes a mystic trilling, the calling of hundreds of birds coming from all directions as the gray bodies mill about, poking at the ground for food. Here and there one flares its wings and hops in the air or runs with wings outstretched. Another bows and tosses a tuft of stubble, then two birds leap together in the air breast to breast. Sandhills mate for life, and the dancing reinforces the pair bond, as well as helping the birds "let off steam." Upon reaching their marshland nesting grounds, they will court in earnest, then spend the summer rearing the chicks. The young migrate with the parents in fall and may still be with them the next spring.

The huge birds are equally mesmerizing as they fly over in trailing flocks, great wings cupping the air, stick legs held out behind. And always there is the eerie, trilling call, the essence of wildness.

When and Where to See Them: A large flock of cranes winters at the Bosque del Apache Wildlife Refuge in New Mexico. Migrating birds appear in the San Luis Valley of Colorado from late February through early April and again from mid-September through November. Nesting sites are localized in Colorado, Utah; Idaho, Montana and Wyoming and in areas of British Columbia, Alberta, the Yukon, Northwest Territories and Alaska.

EYECATCHERS

Once you've heard the eerie trilling of the cranes—*ka-rrooo, ka-rrooo*—it will never leave you. During migration the big, gray birds are easily seen feeding in grain fields or flying overhead in trailing flocks, necks extended and legs held out behind.

Flock of sandhill cranes feeding

Sandhill cranes in flight

Killdeer
A.K.A Killdee, meadow plover

Charadrius vociferus
Family: Plover

This familiar shorebird has a reddishbrown back with reddish rump and tail, white chest and belly, pink legs and two dark neck rings.

Natural History: As the killdeer runs tittering along the water's edge—a round body atop stick legs—it looks like nothing so much as a Victorian lady lifting her skirts and running from an incoming wave. The killdeer is a classic actor, faking injury with a dragging wing, shaky walk and off-kilter body to draw predators, including humans, away from its nest. It lays four eggs directly on rocky soil, its nest at best a scrape in the ground or a collection of pebbles,often in gravel parking lots atop flat-roofed buildings. Young are able to leave the nest soon after hatching and can be seen following their mother around. Killdeer feed on insects and other invertebrates found along the water's edge.

When and Where to See Them: Along lakes, rivers, streams and canals, meadows and farm fields near water. Spring through fall they breed from the southern Rockies into Canada, wintering from New Mexico south. A few birds winter in souther breeding grounds. They are often seen in spring flying high overhead.

EYECATCHERS

The characteristic call from which its name is derived—*kill dee-dee-dee*—as well as its familiar scurry-and-stop run along beaches and streambanks, easily identify the killdeer. In flight it wheels and dives repeatedly while screaming in a high-pitched voice, swooping to skim low across the water's surface.

Killdeer

American Avocet

Recurvirostra americana
Family: Avocet

This distinctive stilt-legged wading bird has striking black-and-white plumage with a graceful, rusty-brown neck and head and long, almost needllike, upcurved bill.

Natural History: Among the shallows an elegant bird moves, bending to dabble in the water, plumed rear thrust out as long, fragile legs carry it through the shallows. Despite a body that seems made of mismatched parts, the avocet is one of the most beautiful birds in nature. Somehow its elegance and grace transcend the plump body set on pencil-thin legs and the absurd upcurving bill projecting from the too-small head.

Surely the avocet was painted by an artist, its plumage deftly colored with bold swatches of black, white and reddish brown. The lines of the bird seem designed to please the eye—the recurved bill, the graceful neck sweeping down to the full body and slim legs.

Bird bills come long and short, slender and fat, straight and sometimes down-curved. So why does the avocet's bill curve up? Wading out in shallow waters, the bird slips its long, narrow bill, which is vertically flattened, below the water surface. Moving at a half-run, the avocet swings its half-opened bill side to side just above the muddy bottom, sweeping up snails, insects and other aquatic invertebrates, occasionally pausing to swallow its catch.

During nesting season, avocets gather in loose colonies, each pair laying eggs in a slight depression in the mud or grass. Despite their stately carriage and reserved manner, avocets become viragos when their nests are threatened, screaming in shrill voices that attract neighboring avocets, all of them ganging up to mob the intruder.

When and Where to See Them: Along shallow ponds, vegetation-lined shorelines and marshy areas at low elevation, mid-March through early November from the southern Rockies into Montana and southern Alberta.

EYECATCHERS

With its upcurving needle bill, orange-brown head and black-and-white body, the avocet can't be confused with any other bird in North America.

American Avocet

Spotted Sandpiper

Actitis macularia

A.K.A. Tip-up, teeter-bob, teeter-tail

Family: Sandpiper

A long-billed shoreline bird, in spring it is gray-brown above with a white underside touched with large, dark spots. The spots disappear in fall and winter. Bill, legs and feet are yellow. A white wing stripe is visible in flight.

Natural History: This shoreline bird common along streams, lakes and reservoirs continually teeters forward and back as if slightly off balance. Its flight is equally offbeat as it flutters for three or four shallow wingbeats, then coasts low over land or water. It can swim and dive and has been known to perch on wires. Spotted sandpipers may nest high in the mountains along streams or lakes.

Spotted sandpipers have an unusual love life for the bird world. Females arrive first on the breeding grounds and compete for arriving males, sometimes battling with other females. They mate with numerous males in one season and defend a territory that may encompass the individual territories of their various mates. The females can lay as many as five clutches of eggs, but are able to hatch and rear all these families only with the help of their mates. These domestic males do most of the brooding of eggs and rearing of young, freeing the females to mate again, lay more eggs and produce more little sandpipers.

When and Where to See Them: Along the shores of lakes and streams throughout the Rockies into northern Canada and Alaska from May to September.

EYECATCHERS

A distinctive habit of repeatedly bobbing forward and back as it dashes jerkily along the shoreline helps identify the spotted sandpiper.

Spotted Sandpiper

Common Snipe
A.K.A. Jack snipe

Gallinago gallinago
Family: Sandpiper

This short-legged sandpiper has an extremely long bill, brownish plumage with lighter stripes and underside and a striped head.

Natural History: On a spring morning or evening in a marshy meadow, an airy whistling fills the sky as a male snipe performs his wonderful courtship flight. Circling, looping and diving endlessly, he produces a marvelous *whoo, whoo* sound that rises and falls in pitch, seeming to come first from one direction, then from another. Called winnowing, this eerie sound isn't a vocalization but a sound produced by air passing through the bird's fanned tail as he dives and loops. Snipe winnow in the morning, evening or during the day if the sky is overcast.

Except when breeding, snipe are solitary and secretive, hiding among the marshland vegetation where they forage for insects, grubs and aquatic invertebrates. They poke their pliable bills straight into vegetation or soft earth, often hunting by feel. Walking through the marsh, you may startle a snipe from its hiding place, the bird rising suddenly from the grass and darting off in erratic flight, shrilly calling *zeep, zeep, zeep.*

Female snipe may mate with several males, becoming monogamous once it's time to build a nest among the marsh grass. The female incubates the eggs but once the young hatch, the adults divide the brood and the male and female care for them separately.

Many people doubt that snipe truly exist, thinking it only a mythical beast greenhorns are sent to capture with a gunny sack—the proverbial snipe hunt.

When and Where to See Them: Spring, summer and fall in marshes, bogs and wet grasslands near water, throughout the Rockies into northern Canada.

EYECATCHERS

The snipe's long bill and short neck will help identify it, but the snipe is so well camouflaged you're likely to see it only if it starts up in front of you. The winnowing courtship flight provides the best opportunity to see a snipe.

Common snipe in hand at a bird banding station

Ring-billed Gull

Larus delawarensis
Family: Gull

This large, handsome white gull displays black-tipped gray wings and a yellow bill with a black ring near the tip. Young birds are a mottled brown.

Natural History: "Sea" gull is the wrong term to use for gulls in the Rockies, since we have large numbers of inland gulls that have never seen the ocean. Ring-billed gulls are familiar plains residents around waterways; you may see them as a bobbing flotilla on the surface of a lake, or as scattered white spots across a moist or flooded field, striding about in a no-nonsense fashion gobbling up insects and worms. They also hang out in the burbs at park ponds, fast-food restaurants and wherever a meal might be scrounged.

Gulls are sociable birds that gather together in big groups to feed and nest. They often switch mates year to year, sometimes taking up with a neighbor from the nest site of the year before. In flight these birds cut the air vigorously with long, slender wings, often spiraling and performing aerial antics.

Gulls eat fish, insects, frogs and the eggs of other birds. In some areas their predation on the nests of shorebirds is a problem, as they are bold and quick to exploit a weaker bird, discovering hidden nests and devouring the eggs.

When and Where to See Them: Common around reservoirs, waterways, and flooded fields on the plains and in western valleys, ring-billed gulls occasionally visit the higher mountains. In summer they breed in the northern Rockies, but are year-round or winter residents of the central and southern Rocky Mountain states.

EYECATCHERS

Listen for the shrill *kee-ha* call of this sleek white gull with gray wings. The bill ring is hard to spot without binoculars and lots of concentration.

Ring-billed Gull

Belted Kingfisher
A.K.A. Lazybird

Ceryle alcyon
Family: Kingfisher

Looking like it's been put together by committee, the kingfisher sports a large, shaggy-crest on its blue head, a heavy, stabbing bill, a stubby tail and short legs. The back and wing plumage is blue with a blue band across the white breast. The female has a second, chestnut-colored chest band.

Natural History: The loud, rattling call of the kingfisher will greet you along a stream course just before the bird passes by. Though not a waterbird, this bird earned its name as "king of the fishers" for its aggressive fishing style. It may fly just above the water's surface and dive in when it spots fish; dive from a perch or vantage point on a streamside limb; or fly high up, hover, then swoop down and hit the water's surface, using its bill to pluck prey from the water. The adults teach their young to fish by dropping bits of food in the water for them to retrieve.

Always found around water, kingfishers can be seen sitting alone on perches above lakes and streams. They nest in burrows dug as much as fifteen feet into riverbanks. The floor of the burrow entrance has two grooves created by the birds dragging their feet each time they enter.

When and Where to See Them: Along streams, lakes and canals throughout the year in the southern Rockies, into British Columbia and Alberta spring through fall.

EYECATCHERS

A bird perched streamside or flying low over the water, with a "punk-cut" blue crest, oversized head and rattling call, is unmistakably a belted kingfisher.

Belted Kingfisher female

Red-winged Blackbird

A.K.A. Red-wing

Agelaius phoeniceus

Family: Troupial

The male is a glossy black with bold scarlet wing patches edged with yellow. The drab female is brownish and blends well into cattails and marsh vegetation.

Natural History: A marsh during spring is the best place to make the acquaintance of red-winged blackbirds. The males stake out territories among the cattails and tules, proclaiming their turf with clamorous song, the cumulative result a cacophony of birdsong that fills the marsh with noise and life.

The females arrive after the males, secretively setting up their own territories, then seeking out a mate. If the male isn't interested he will drive the female away. In colonies with more females than males, the males may mate with numerous female neighbors. While they share marshy nesting grounds with their cousin, the yellow-headed blackbird, red-wings nest at the edges of ponds and occasionally on the ground, not over water like the yellow-heads. Listen for the redwing's buzzing *konk-a-reee* call.

Crowds of blackbirds will mob and dive-bomb intruders (including humans) who venture into their marshy territories, sometimes pursuing and harassing marsh hawks and other aerial predators. In late summer and fall, after the young are on the wing, blackbirds gather in big flocks—the males in one group, the females and young in another—and leave the marsh by day to feed in meadows and grain fields.

When and Where to See Them: Look for red-winged blackbirds among thick vegetation around freshwater marshes, flooded fields and riparian areas. Year-round residents of the southern Rockies, in spring and summer they spread throughout the Rockies into northern Canada for breeding.

EYECATCHERS

The bright scarlet chevrons on the wings of the male identify this handsome blackbird.

Red-winged Blackbird male

Red-winged Blackbird female

Yellow-headed Blackbird

Xanthocephalus xanthocephalus

A.K.A. Saffron-headed maizo bird, yellow-heads

Family: Troupial

The male yellow-headed blackbird has a striking yellow head and breast, and wing patches that flash white in flight. The female is a drab brown with a little yellow on the throat.

Natural History: Where there are cattail marshes, there are likely to be yellow-headed blackbirds. Sitting atop bobbing cattails like bright yellow ornaments among the green vegetation, the territorial males survey their domain, toes wrapped around the stalks, sometimes practically spread-eagled between two different cattails. Throwing their heads back, their open bills making a V against the sky, the yellow-heads let out a rasping, unmusical call, sounding like a rusty, protesting hinge. The raucous, croaking *klee, klee, ko, kow* is noticeably different from that of their cousin the red-winged blackbird.

Though both blackbirds nest in colonies among the reeds and cattails, the yellow-heads usually choose a site over water. Males arrive first in the spring, squabbling among each other as they set up nesting territories. Yellow-heads will drive red-wings from certain areas of the marsh. After mating, the female weaves her nest of wet reeds and grasses, using plant stalks as supports. As the grasses dry, they draw the nest tight and secure to the supporting stalks. If the supporting plants grow at different speeds, the carefully built nest may begin to tilt and the hard-working female must build a new one.

When and Where to See Them: In spring, summer and fall on marshy wetlands throughout the Rockies into central Canada. Some birds winter in more southern breeding grounds.

EYECATCHERS

Watch for a glossy black bird with bright yellow head sitting among the cattails.

Male yellow-headed blackbird singing

Female yellow-headed blackbird

Male yellow-headed blackbird

Common Yellowthroat

A.K.A. Black-masked warbler,
ground warbler

Geothlypis trichas

Family: American wood warbler

This small, olive-green warbler hides behind a black facemask, brow stripe and bright yellow throat and breast. The olive-drab female lacks the mask but has some yellow on the throat.

Natural History: Visit any marshy area or shrubby vegetation near water in summer and you'll likely notice the yellowthroat, a spot of yellow darting amongst the greenery. This bird is often called a ground warbler because of its discreet habit of slipping in and out of its nest on the ground and scurrying a distance through the undergrowth before taking flight. To avoid being seen by predators while bringing food home to their hatchlings, the parents sneak into their nests through the grass, feed the young, and creep back out again.

But like most birds, the male yellowthroat gives itself away with its urge to sing. Sitting on the tips of cattails or tules near its marshy home, the male comes out of hiding and breaks into song—a perky, repetitive tune described as *whitichy, whitichy,* sometimes repeated 250 times an hour. It may emerge indignantly when a visitor enters its territory, railing at the intruder with scolding chirps and chatter, then darting nervously about the foliage before slipping away again.

Yellowthroats are one of the three most common birds parasitized by cowbirds, larger birds that lay their eggs in the warbler's nests to be raised by the smaller birds.

When and Where to See Them: In cattail marshes, shrub thickets and marshy areas throughout the Rockies from spring through fall.

EYECATCHERS

The yellowthroat's black Lone Ranger facemask and bright yellow throat flashing among green foliage reveal its identity.

Common yellowthroat male singing

Birds of the Mountains

Turkey Vulture
Golden Eagle
White-tailed Ptarmigan
Broad-tailed Hummingbird
Red-naped Sapsucker
Tree Swallow
Gray Jay
Steller's Jay
Clark's Nutcracker
Common Raven
Mountain Chickadee
Pygmy Nuthatch
American Dipper
Mountain Bluebird
Wilson's Warbler
Western Tanager
Black-headed Grosbeak
White-crowned Sparrow
Dark-eyed Junco
Pine Siskin

Turkey Vulture

A.K.A. Turkey buzzard, carrion crow, John crow

Cathartes aura

Family: American vulture

A large, black hawk-like bird with a six-foot wingspan, the vulture has a small, naked red head.

Natural History: Despite its homely, naked red head, distasteful role as a carrion eater, and reputation as a portent of death, the turkey vulture is a prince of the air, sailing for hours on the rising thermals, either alone or in groups of up to a dozen. Watching these birds spiraling higher in the sky till they disappear in the heavens, it's no wonder some Indian tribes thought them messengers of the gods.

To become airborne, the vulture takes a few ungainly bounds, flapping intently, but once in the air becomes a graceful aerialist. Vultures cruise in circles, rarely flapping as they ride columns of rising warm air. How are they able to stay aloft so long? Their six-foot wings provide a large gliding surface compared to their body size, allowing their bodies to fall at a rate slower than the rising air. Vultures maintain their glide by spreading the primaries, or "fingertips," of their wings to reduce drag.

Though their habit of scavenging for dead animals is repugnant to humans, vultures play an essential role in the ecosystem, helping recycle nutrients locked up in the bodies of other animals. As scavengers they are at the top of the food chain and have suffered poisoning from DDT and pesticides concentrated in the food they eat.

Unlike many birds, turkey vultures have an excellent sense of smell, which they may use in locating food, although research indicates they forage at altitudes too high to carry scent to them from the ground. Their incredibly keen eyesight is likely the main tool for finding food.

When and Where to See Them: In open, arid country, woodlands, farms and grasslands, vultures live year-round in the southern Rockies, moving up through the Rockies into southern Canada for spring, summer and fall.

EYECATCHERS

Overhead the turkey vulture, a great dark bird cruising endlessly on the thermals, can be differentiated from a golden eagle by its smaller head, lighter trailing edges of the wings and the way it holds its wings up slightly in a V, rocking a little side to side as it soars.

Turkey Vulture (photographed in captivity)

Golden Eagle
A.K.A. Mountain eagle, ring-tailed eagle, royal eagle

Aquila chrysaetos
Family: Hawk

A large, brown eagle with lighter golden-brown nape, the golden has a smaller beak and head than the bald eagle and a longer tail. The immature birds display a white band at the base of the tail. Unlike the bald eagle, the golden's legs are feathered down to the feet.

Natural History: A great, brown eagle soars among canyons and cliffs like a messenger from the gods. More than the bald, the golden eagle symbolized power and majesty to many cultures. Native Americans valued their feathers as symbols of strength, and in Europe only royalty could fly eagles for falconing.

How fitting that this large, powerful eagle inhabits wild mountain ledges and rock promontories. From high, rocky vantages they survey their vast territory, keeping an eye out for danger and opportunity, launching out onto the thermals to soar and hunt, lighting easily on the cliff's edge upon their return.

Observing golden eagles on the hunt is a thrill—they circle in the air, pausing as they spot prey invisible to human eyes, then close their wings and plummet upon the victim, making the kill with sharp talons. Golden eagles are active and diverse hunters, preying on everything from insects to fish to deer fawns. Rodents are a main food source and eagle predation is an important control for rodent and rabbit populations. They will also eat carrion.

The golden eagle pair mates for life, hunting and defending a territory averaging thirty-six square miles, to which they return each year to nest. They lay two eggs and after hatching, the larger nestling usually kills the smaller, ensuring the survivor of undistracted parental attention.

Like bald eagles, the golden's voice, when heard, is a weak mewing with occasional yelps and squeals.

When and Where to See Them: Golden eagles reside year-round in mountainous, plains-canyon or hilly terrain to the edge of the alpine zone throughout the Rockies.

EYECATCHERS

The great size of the golden identifies it as an eagle. The lack of white head and the golden's preference for mountain and dryland habitat, as opposed to water, separate it from the bald eagle.

114

Golden Eagle

White-tailed Ptarmigan

Lagopus leucurus
Family: Grouse

The white-tailed ptarmigan is a plump-bodied, small-headed grouse that in winter is snow white and in summer has mottled brown plumage with white underparts.

Natural History: Ptarmigan are mirrors of the seasons above timberline. Beautifully designed to change colors as their environment transforms, they wear mottled brown in summer that makes them indistinguishable against a backdrop of rocky tundra, then gradually turn white with the coming of the snow. By winter they are all white except for eyes, bill and claws; they even grow feathery "snowshoes" on their feet that help them get around on the snow. Intrepid alpine residents, ptarmigan neither hibernate nor migrate to avoid the ravages of winter, but stay year-round on the forbidding land above timberline. Like other grouse, the male ptarmigan struts and calls during courtship, but his display is not as dramatic as the booming dance of prairie-chickens or sage grouse. Ptarmigan build their nests in the open or under a shrub, lining a shallow depression with grass, lichen and feathers. Sitting tightly upon her nest, the female is incredibly well hidden by her protective coloration and will likely not be noticed until literally stumbled over.

Ptarmigan depend on the alpine willows, feeding on the buds, shoots, leaves and flowers, and finding shelter beneath them. In winter, ptarmigan burrow into soft snowdrifts, the snow acting as insulation against wind and cold. Researchers are concerned that ptarmigan populations may be declining due to diminishing habitat. Big game animals, forced to stay higher and longer in the alpine zone as human development encroaches on their lower altitude wintering grounds, graze and trample the willows ptarmigan depend upon.

When and Where to See Them: Ptarmigan live year-round in alpine regions throughout the Rockies, inhabiting rocky alpine slopes and mountain meadows.

EYECATCHERS

Unless you're extremely sharp-eyed, you will likely only see ptarmigan when they flush practically from underfoot and flutter off across the tundra to settle a safe distance away.

White-tailed ptarmigan male in summer plumage (wearing leg bands)

White-tailed ptarmigan in winter plumage (seven birds)

Broad-tailed Hummingbird
A.K.A. Hummer

Selasphorus platycercus

Family: Hummingbird

This tiny bird measures about four inches long with a long, needle-like bill. The back and wings are iridescent green and the underside is whitish. The male has a red throat.

Natural History: "What's that?!" will probably be your response when first you make the acquaintance of a hummingbird. Buzzing like shrill green bullets, they zip about looking for likely flowers to feed on, pausing to hover as if thinking things over, then speeding off again. Hummingbirds are themselves like brilliantly colored blossoms come to life as they dart among the bright mountain flowers on a sunny summer day.

Watch hummers as they gather around a feeder or other food source. Like a cluster of humming emeralds, they dart and hover, dart and hover. The dominant bird will spend lots of energy driving others away from the food.

Hummingbirds have been recorded flying and hovering at between twenty-two and seventy-nine wingbeats per second, with a record 200 beats during courtship flights of some species. Their frenetic pace would wear out a human in no time—a 170-pound man would require 155,000 calories a day to match the hummer's activity. The hummingbird's aerodynamic control is also amazing—hovering motionless, flying backward and changing direction by making barrel rolls. Some species of hummingbird migrate 2,000 miles from their breeding grounds to wintering sites in Central and South America. Imagine how many wingbeats on tiny wings it takes to fly so far!

Wonderfully adapted to feed on flower nectar, hummers have a hollow, straw-like tongue that works like a pump to suck nectar from deep within flowers. But while the hummer is an incredible flier, its tiny legs and feet are so undeveloped it can hardly walk.

When and Where to See Them: From early May through mid-September in meadows and flowering areas of mountain conifer and aspen forests of the central and southern Rockies.

EYECATCHERS

A tiny, iridescent green blur of activity among the mountain willows and wildflowers, and the humming trill of their wings, usually announce the arrival of the broad-tailed hummingbird.

Broad-tailed Hummingbird male

Red-naped Sapsucker
A.K.A Yellow-bellied sapsucker

Sphyrapicus nuchalis
Family: Woodpecker

This black-and-white-backed woodpecker has a red forehead, throat and nape and wide black-and-white stripes on the side of the head.

Natural History: Seeking sap and the soft, inner bark of trees, sapsuckers drill orderly rows of holes in live trees, frequently willows, sometimes making a checkerboard pattern. Unlike other woodpeckers that have a barbed tongue to hook insects, sapsuckers have a brushy tongue they use to lick up the sap that runs out of the holes they drill, thereby eating the insects trapped in the sticky tree resin. Far from injuring the tree, the bird's foraging removes bark beetles and other insects that damage or kill timber. Sapsuckers defend their "sap wells" from neighbors—hummingbirds, squirrels, chipmunks and other birds. They prefer the sap from deciduous trees like aspen, but will eat pine pitch.

Sapsuckers also prefer deciduous trees for nesting and will return to the same tree every year, though they often drill new holes. This habit of excavating a new home each year is important in providing nest holes for other cavity nesters that can't drill their own.

The mated sapsucker pair taps out a duet on the tree bark and performs a ritual tapping at the nest entrance. Using the materials at hand, the adults line the nest with wood chips. When the young are able to leave the nest, they are taught the fine art of sapsucking by their parents.

Once considered to be the Rocky Mountain version of the yellow-bellied sapsucker, the red-naped is now classified as a separate species.

When and Where to See Them: In aspen or other deciduous mountain forests throughout the Rockies from spring through fall. They migrate to the south-western United States and into western Mexico for winter.

EYECATCHERS

The red patches on forehead, throat and neck identify this black-and-white woodpecker. Listen for its drumming in aspen groves and mountain woodlands, where it is usually the only woodpecker.

Red-naped sapsucker with food for nestlings

Tree Swallow

Tachycineta bicolor

A.K.A. White-bellied swallow, white-breasted swallow   Family: Swallow

This round-headed bird has an iridescent, almost metallic, blue back, white underparts and a slightly forked tail.

Natural History: In the world of swallows, tree swallows are mavericks. While other swallows live in busy, crowded colonies reminiscent of apartment complexes filled with birds, tree swallows form only loose colonies, sometimes inhabiting mailboxes or birdhouses. They usually nest near water in a tree cavity, competing with other cavity nesters for homes (nest boxes have helped increase swallow numbers). Tree swallows have a more versatile diet than other swallows. They eat berries and seeds while other swallows are strict insect eaters. Being less limited in food choice, tree swallows are able to arrive earlier in the spring on northern nesting grounds and stay later in the fall.

Swallows are amazing aerial acrobats, snapping up flying insects, changing direction abruptly to grab a meal. Returning to their nests they may fly right in the entry hole without pausing.

Before migrating they gather in huge flocks, flying in to roost at night in a dark, milling mass. At times flocks of thousands of birds may fill the sky, twisting and wheeling like one great being before settling down for the night.

The tree swallow is often confused with the violet-green swallow, a similar swallow that has a greener back and white patches on the lower back.

When and Where to See Them: From April to early October in the mountains up to timberline throughout the Rockies, especially in wooded habitat near water. In spring and fall they linger on the plains.

EYECATCHERS

The tree swallow looks like a line was drawn down its length from mouth to tail and it was painted shiny blue above the line and white below.

Tree swallow outside entrance to nest cavity

Tree Swallow

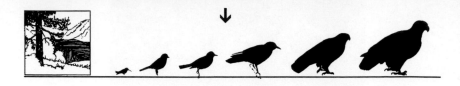

Gray Jay
Perisoreus canadensis

A.K.A. Camp robber, Canada jay, whiskey jack
Family: Crow

The brazen gray jay is fluffy gray with white throat, forehead and underside, and a dark nape. Young are charcoal gray all over.

Natural History: Anyone who has picnicked in the mountains has likely made the acquaintance of the gray jay. This bold opportunist is quite curious and will approach very close seeking food, even stealing tidbits from the picnic table, after which it slips away to secrecy. Tales of the jay's boldness as a thief are endless—it enters tents, snatches bacon from frying pans, steals bait from traps, even learns to come at the sound of a gunshot in the chance of raiding a game carcass. Gray jays feed on insects, berries, carrion, mice or whatever they can find. They cache food, using a sticky saliva to glue tidbits in a crevice or other hiding place.

Gray jays travel in family groups and arrive in marauding flocks, landing on the lower branches of trees, then hopping higher and higher seeking a vantage point before sailing down to another tree. The gray jay nests in late March in coniferous forests, incubating its eggs dutifully even as the snow of a late spring storm falls on its back. The nest is shaped like an upside down umbrella, very well insulated with feathers and moss. Because the gray jay does not migrate and lives in the high mountains, it is thickly insulated with feathers, hence its fluffy appearance.

When and Where to See Them: During the summer gray jays are almost always seen in groups at campgrounds, picnic areas and cabins in foothills and mountain coniferous forests throughout the Rockies. They winter at lower elevations where they may visit foothills birdfeeders.

EYECATCHERS

More identifiable by its bold behavior than its appearance, the gray jay will show up wherever tidbits of food may be begged or stolen from humans.

Gray Jay

Steller's Jay
A.K.A. Mountain blue jay

Cyanocitta stelleri
Family: Crow

The Steller's jay is a handsome, very blue mountain jay with a black head and crest.

Natural History: If you find yourself in a pine forest in the Rockies, you'll soon meet a bold and handsome bird dressed in blue—the Steller's jay. Though a little shyer than their close relatives the gray jays, Steller's jays are quick to move in on a picnic looking for tidbits. Open a picnic basket and the trees around you will soon fill with jays; characteristically, they land on the lower limbs of trees, work their way up to the top, then fly down to another tree.

Steller's are the only jays in the Rockies that have a crest (gray and scrub jays have a rounded head). Visitors unfamiliar with this mountain jay frequently mistakenly call them blue jays. This jay's common name, "Steller," comes from the name of a well-known biologist, not from the word "stellar," meaning starry or outstanding.

Steller's jays eat mainly pine nuts and vegetable matter, but about a third of their diet is meat—insects, invertebrates and the eggs and nestlings of other birds.

The call of the Steller's jay, a common sound in mountain forests, is harsh and sometimes quarrelsome. These jays will mimic the scream of a red-tailed hawk or golden eagle, perhaps to frighten smaller birds from their nests, leaving the eggs and young open to attack. By contrast, when around their own nests they are quiet and retiring.

When and Where to See Them: In ponderosa pine and scrub oak forests of the mountains and foothills throughout the Rockies, ranging up to higher altitude spruce/fir habitat. They are a year-round mountain resident.

EYECATCHERS

Watch for this striking blue jay with the black crest as it flies from ground to stump to tree limb, especially around a picnic site. Its harsh *ack, ack, ack . . .* call will often announce its presence.

126

Steller's Jay

Clark's Nutcracker

Nucifraga columbiana
Family: Crow

The Clark's nutcracker is a large, gray bird with a long beak. Its wings, tail, legs and bill are black. The edges of the tail and wing patches are white.

Natural History: The nutcracker's raucous voice and bold behavior label it a member of the crow family. Named after Captain William Clark of the Lewis and Clark expedition, the boisterous and gregarious nutcracker lives year-round in the mountains, moving from summer breeding grounds in high-altitude forests to lower elevations in winter. It feeds on pine nuts, seeds and occasional insects and small mammals. In summer and fall it caches food for winter on south-facing slopes, finding the food again by memory. Nutcrackers range widely searching for food, their presence directly related to the abundance of pine cones in an area. They breed very early, in March or April, when the snow is still deep on the ground in their mountain homes.

Nutcrackers have a special pouch under their tongues that lets them carry dozens of pine seeds in their mouths. The birds hold the seeds with their toes, using their long beaks to crack them open. Individuals are either right-or left-"handed."

Nutcrackers are important in the dispersal of whitebark pines. After gathering the seeds from the soft cones in late summer, the birds cache the seeds in mountain meadows. Though they mark the sites with twigs and pebbles, they forget to return to many of the sites, allowing the pines to germinate.

When and Where to See Them: At high elevation and timberline picnic areas in summer, lower elevations in winter from New Mexico through southern British Columbia. You won't see this bird commonly, but when you do, there will be a bunch of them.

EYECATCHERS

If you're picnicking in a high altitude coniferous forest, this big gray and black bird will find you, land in a nearby tree and beg to share your meal. Its loud, gravelly *kraaaw kraaaw* call often announces its presence.

Clark's Nutcracker

Common Raven

Corvus corax
Family: Crow

A large, glossy black bird with a powerful bill, the raven is larger than a crow and has a wedge-shaped tail. Up close the raven has a feathery ruff around its neck.

Natural History: Ravens are a common sight in the clear blue mountain sky, soaring like black specters, their shadows raking the ground, or lighting in the tops of trees to survey their domain. Though ravens look like hawks at a distance, their smaller, more pointed heads help distinguish them. Gliding ravens hold their outstretched wings flat, unlike crows and some hawks whose wings angle slightly upward.

Ravens light in the tops of trees, their raucous calls echoing across the mountain valleys and forests like the voices of mountain kings. One of their calls sounds like someone knocking loudly on hollow wood.

Like its crow cousins, ravens are opportunistic feeders, taking advantage of any potential food, from garbage to carrion. They may prey on small mammals, birds and insects. Ravens seem good at "thinking out" solutions to problems, especially when figuring how to get to food! They have been observed dropping rocks on shellfish to crack them open as well as caching food to be eaten later.

Ravens aren't as gregarious as crows and are often seen alone or in pairs. They form long-term bonds, staying with the same mate over several years. If you're lucky you may see them "playing" together in the air, performing spectacular aerial loops and dives. Ravens tend to nest on hard-to-reach rocky ledges out of reach of predators.

To the Plains Indians ravens were important spirit animals, often thought to be omens of good luck, bearers of news or storytellers. The next time you're in the mountains and a raven lights in a tree near you, see if you don't feel like he knows something you don't!

When and Where to See Them: Year-round in mountains, foothills and rugged country throughout the United States and Canadian Rockies.

EYECATCHERS

The loud, raspy *raa-aa!* echoing across a mountain valley may clue you to the raven's presence, and once you see this large, handsome black bird riding the thermals on a warm day, you won't mistake it.

130

Common Raven

Mountain Chickadee

Parus gambeli
Family: Titmouse

This short-billed little gray bird displays a white underside, a black-capped head with a white stripe above the eye, and a black throat bib.

Natural History: Chickadees are such busy little birds they must consume their weight in food each day to fuel their furnace. They eat spiders and their eggs, insects and seeds. Chickadees nest in tree holes, often taking over an abandoned woodpecker hole, which they line with moss, fur, feathers or shredded bark to make a soft nest.

When incubating eggs, the female is very protective and intolerant of being disturbed. If bothered she lunges and makes a snake-like hiss at intruders.

With a black cap and throat bib, mountain chickadees are similar in appearance to their familiar cousin the black-capped chickadee, echoing the characteristic *chick-a-dee-dee-dee* call. They whistle a high, clear song easily heard in the mountain forest—*fee-bee*—with the first note higher than the second.

In winter, chickadees band together in flocks with other species; studies have shown that in these mixed flocks the alert chickadees act as sentinels for other birds.

When and Where to See Them: Year-round residents throughout the Rockies, chickadees summer in foothills and mountain coniferous forests up to timber-line, moving in winter to open woodlands, groves along streams and out onto the plains.

EYECATCHERS

A small sparrowlike bird with black bib and cap, the mountain chickadee moves busily among the spruces and pines of the mountain forests. Its whistly call is easily heard.

Mountain Chickadee

Pygmy Nuthatch
A.K.A. Black-eared nuthatch

Sitta pygmaea
Family: Common nuthatch

This little bird has a slate-gray back and wings, whitish breast, short tail, small head and a strong, long, pointed bill.

Natural History: These busy little inhabitants of the pine forest fly in flocks from tree to tree, the members of the group scurrying up and down the bark and around tree limbs in search of insects. They call constantly, their piping voices an excited chattering.

The male and female nuthatch stay together for several seasons, often helped out in "child rearing" by unmated male helpers—usually their young from the year before or the brothers of the mated pair. Couples with helpers produce more young than those parenting alone.

Nuthatches will stay in their forest territories year-round, caching pine nuts to eat when other food is scarce. The name "nuthatch" comes from their habit of breaking nuts into pieces and wedging them into crevices in tree bark. When winter arrives they gather in groups to forage and hang out together in tree holes and other nest cavities. One nuthatch gang estimated at 150 birds was found roosting together in a hollow pine. From the outside the old tree had many entrance holes, but they all opened onto one big room filled with roosting nuthatches!

When and Where to See Them: In mountain coniferous forests, primarily ponderosa pine, year-round, from the southern Rockies into southern British Columbia.

EYECATCHERS

Look for a little gray bird clinging vertically to a tree trunk. If it's hanging upside down or coming down the bark headfirst, you've spotted a nuthatch.

Pygmy nuthatch at its nesting cavity

American Dipper
A.K.A. Water ouzel

Cinclus mexicanus
Family: Dipper

The dipper, a soot-gray bird with short tail and long legs, resembles a starling, without the speckles.

Natural History: You're watching a rather nondescript gray bird along the edge of a stream, when suddenly it walks into the water and disappears!

The dipper may startle first-time observers with its predilection for underwater exploration—dippers not only walk underwater, they "fly," propelling themselves through the water with strong wingbeats. They can dive as deep as twenty feet, walking on the stream bottom against a strong current.

The dipper is well adapted to hunting underwater. It has a large oil gland for waterproofing its dense feathers. This preen gland is about ten times the size of those of other songbirds. A scaly flap over the nostrils keeps out water, while a third eyelid allows the bird to see underwater while keeping debris out of the eye.

Dippers are often seen standing on a rock at the edge of a rushing mountain stream, bobbing continuously. They may wade in the water with only their heads submerged, gobbling up aquatic insects, larvae, fish fry or whatever food swims by. Or they may make a more dramatic entrance, "crash diving" into a stream from a rock or even from flight.

Dippers are mavericks in other ways. They don't migrate, but may move to lower elevations if streams freeze up. They sing year-round, a clear, loud bubbling song audible over the rushing of the stream. The bulky, oven-shaped nest has a side entrance and may be built on a rock in the middle of a rushing stream or under a waterfall.

When and Where to See Them: Dippers like clear, rushing water. Look for them along high mountain streams throughout the Rockies in June, July and August. In winter, dippers migrate to lower elevations, in foothills or on the plains close to the mountains, seeking free-flowing streams and waterways.

EYECATCHERS

This bird bobs constantly and walks underwater.

American Dipper

Mountain Bluebird

Sialia currucoides
Family: Thrush

The male mountain bluebird is a startling bright blue, the color of the sky. The breast is somewhat lighter than the wings. The female is brownish gray.

Natural History: When you first glimpse a mountain bluebird, you may think it's a scrap of bright blue cloth snagged on a fencewire or a bit of blue paper skittering across a mountain meadow. The color of the summer sky, bluebirds blossom on fences along mountain highways, in meadows and mountain parks, brightening the summer day. As soon as the young are able to leave the nest, bluebirds flock together and head for the high mountains, fluttering in waves of blue up mountain slopes and onto the alpine tundra. Mountain bluebirds differ from other bluebirds by their preference for more open habitat.

Mountain bluebirds nest in holes in trees or other structures, using either natural cavities or nests excavated by woodpeckers. Removal of dead timber in forests and replacement of wood fenceposts with metal has reduced the nesting sites for bluebirds, who must compete with other bird species— sparrows, flickers, starlings—for nest cavities. Artificial nest boxes are an important replacement for nest sites lost in natural habitat.

Primarily an insect-eater, the mountain bluebird may launch suddenly from its perch to pluck a flying insect from the air, or hunt by watching for prey on the ground as it flies, hovering when it spots something, then dropping down to grab a meal.

While the mountain bluebird is all blue, the eastern and western bluebirds have sky-blue backs and red breasts.

When and Where to See Them: The mountain bluebird is mainly a summer visitor to the Rockies, inhabiting foothills, sagelands and mountain meadows up to timberline throughout the United States Rockies into central Canada from March through October. Some are resident in the southern Rockies

---

EYECATCHERS

Watch for these bright blue birds sitting on fencewires or flashing across mountain meadows in late spring and summer.

Mountain Bluebird female

Mountain Bluebird male

Wilson's Warbler

Wilsonia pusilla

A.K.A. Wilson's blackcap, black-capped warbler, pileolated warbler

Family: American wood warbler

The Wilson's is a small warbler with olive-green back and wings and yellow underside. The male has a large, black cap; the female has a small one or sometimes none at all.

Natural History: The energetic Wilson's warbler flits around the outer foliage of shrubs and trees, snapping up flying insects like a shopper after bargains at a fifty-percent-off sale. Its yellow breast flashes brightly among the greenery. At times it falls into excited bouts of tail twitching, rotating its tail in a circle and repeatedly flipping its wings. The warbler's song is an excited chattering that matches its frenetic personality.

During migration Wilson's warblers may visit urban parks and foliage, but they prefer to nest in the stratified air of the high mountains, even at elevations of 10,000 feet or more. They build their grassy, ball-like nests on the ground or in the lower branches of willow thickets and boggy areas along high mountain lakes and streams. They bring a frantic energy to the willow thickets, in keeping perhaps with the brief but brilliant burst of summertime life at high altitude.

When and Where to See Them: In April and May migrating warblers abound along prairie waterways. They move to high-altitude nest sites in marshy thickets, bogs and moist woodlands of the central and northern Rockies when winter fades from the mountains.

EYECATCHERS

Watch for a bright yellow warbler with black cap flitting among the outer branches of trees and shrubs. Listen for the male's bursts of spring song, a series of accelerating twits—*chit, chit, chit, chit.*

Wilson's Warbler female

Western Tanager

Piranga ludoviciana
Family: Tanager

The male western tanager is a beautiful songbird with a bright yellow body, bright red head and black wings, back and tail. The female is a dull olive yellow and lacks the red head.

Natural History: "Did you see that bird?!" is the usual delighted response to the first sighting of a western tanager. A flash of red, yellow and black in the mountain forest, this showy tanager is a bird right out of the paint box.

The song of the tanager carries through the scrub forest, sounding like a hoarse robin. In spring and early summer, tanagers feed on insects in the upper canopy of the forest but by late summer switch to berries, buds and other forest fruits. Sometimes their aerial insect pursuit is acrobatic—they shoot straight up after a meal or flash through the foliage like rainbows run amok.

Tanagers usually nest in scrub oak, pinyon-juniper and ponderosa pine forests in the foothills, building fragile saucerlike nests of grass, weeds and bark in a branch fork far out from the trunk. Once on the nest the drab female sits tight, rarely flushing. Hunting among the high tree branches, the male is seen less often during nesting season, though his song reveals his presence and gives away the nesting site.

When and Where to See Them: Tanagers arrive in late spring in wooded areas along prairie streams, lower valleys and urban areas. By early summer they move to their foothills and lower mountain nesting grounds in coniferous forests throughout the Rockies. In fall they reverse the process, moving through lower elevation wooded areas before heading south in late September.

EYECATCHERS

This flashy yellow-and-black bird with the red head will not just catch your eye but knock your socks off.

Western Tanager male

Black-headed Grosbeak

A.K.A. Rocky Mountain grosbeak

Pheucticus melanocephalus

Family: Finch

A plump, orange songbird with a heavy, whitish bill, the male has a black head, black-and-white tail and wings and a yellow belly. The female is buffy with black streaks on the head and back, and white stripes around the eyes.

Natural History: The male black-headed grosbeak sits on the uppermost twig of a tree, its black head and orange plumage in bright contrast to the blue sky, singing a clear, whistling song much like a robin's. One male was observed performing nonstop for seven hours.

This big-beaked bird favors deciduous woodlands, streamside thickets and pond edges. It builds a loose, bulky nest of twigs and weeds. A determined homeowner, the female will fiercely drive other grosbeaks from her territory. Parental duties are shared by her mate, who helps incubate the eggs and feed the hatchlings. The birds may be rather secretive when they have young in the nest. The black-headed grosbeak sometimes interbreeds with its eastern counterpart, the rose-breasted grosbeak, where their ranges overlap.

Grosbeaks have a diverse diet, eating fruits, insects and occasionally visiting picnic sites in deciduous forests to scrounge for crumbs.

When and Where to See Them: Black-headed grosbeaks are found late spring through early fall in open woodlands, mountain wooded areas along waterways as well as orchards and gardens throughout the United States Rockies into southern British Columbia.

EYECATCHERS

The male's bright orange breast and black head distinguish it, while the fat, sturdy beak identifies these birds as grosbeaks, literally "large beak."

Black-headed Grosbeak male

White-crowned Sparrow

Zonotrichia leucophrys
Family: Finch

This medium-sized brownish sparrow has rusty colored wings and a black head striped from front to back with white.

Natural History: These perky sparrows crowd lower-elevation feeders in spring till the snow melts in the high country, when they move to the mountains. They like to build their nests in willowy areas around lakes and moist bogs or on the alpine tundra among dwarf stands of Engelmann spruce and subalpine fir, where they can feed in open, grassy areas and flee to the shrubs for protection. Their nests are usually low in a tree or bush, sometimes right on the ground, and one sparrow pair may raise as many as four clutches of eggs in a season.

Perching on a twig above the shrubs that hide its nest, the male sparrow announces its territory with a loud, whistling melody. Different sparrow song "dialects" have been recorded and vary from region to region. Unlike many birds, white-crowned sparrows sing even at night.

A study of the importance of the sparrow's head stripes found that birds with the brightest black-and-white stripes had the highest dominance, while those with duller stripes, typical of juvenile birds, were at the bottom of the totem pole. When researchers used paint to brighten up the feathers of dull-headed birds, the birds' status among their fellow sparrows went up accordingly.

When and Where to See Them: White-crowns favor open woodlands, brushy grasslands, parks and roadsides. Many are frequent winter visitors at low-elevation birdfeeders. They breed throughout the Rockies and are year-round residents of the southern Rockies. From mid-April through mid-autumn, they move from plains to foothills to high mountains, visiting the alpine zone during mid-summer.

EYECATCHERS

The black-and-white striped "helmet" on the head identifies this otherwise gray-brown sparrow.

White-crowned Sparrow male

Immature White-crowned Sparrow

Dark-eyed Junco

A.K.A. Snow bird, Oregon junco, slate-colored junco, white-winged junco, gray-headed junco

Junco hyemalis
Family: Finch

There are four races of dark-eyed junco, each varying in coloration. The *Oregon* form has a dark, blue-gray hood covering its head and upper chest, rust-brown back, rosy sides, and gray wings and tail. The *gray-headed* has a light-gray head and sides and reddishbrown back. The *slate-colored* junco lacks the red color and is slate gray all over except for a white belly. *White-winged* juncos are similar to slate-colored but have white wing bars, more white in the tail, and are larger than the others. All juncos have white-edged tails.

Natural History: Once thought to be four different species, the different races of dark-eyed junco have now been combined by biologists into one species because, despite apparent differences, they interbreed—proof of the complete lack of respect birds have for our need to classify them.

In early spring juncos move from their winter homes on the prairie and lower foothills, abandoning birdfeeders for the emerging plants and buds of the mountains. Arriving in mountain coniferous forests, the males set up territories, locate a prominent perch and announce their presence to the world with song. Juncos usually build their soft, grassy cup nests in shallow depressions in the ground protected by a shrub or other overhang. A foraging flock of juncos may spread out in the woods looking for food, keeping in touch by calling constantly.

Once the young are out of the nest, junco families move in flocks even higher into the mountains to take advantage of the brief abundance of the alpine bloom. When winter storms arrive to end their summer idyll, the juncos filter back down to their winter range on the plains.

When and Where to See Them: In winter in the lower foothills and prairies and at backyard feeders of the south and central Rockies, into southern British Columbia and Alberta. From mid-May till late September they move into the mountains and up into northern Canada, breeding in coniferous forests and mixed woodlands, with occasional forays above timberline. White-winged juncos are found primarily in the Black Hills.

EYECATCHERS

Watch for the junco's white tail edges, visible in flight. Each race has its own identifying patterns of coloration.

Dark-eyed Junco male—gray-headed race

Pine Siskin

A.K.A. Pine finch, pine linnet, gray linnet

Carduelis pinus
Family: Finch

Unremarkable gray-brown birds with buffy underparts, dark streaking and yellow on wings and tail, siskins are most noticeable as a twittering flock flies overhead in the mountains.

Natural History: On a typical summer day in the mountains the pines are alive with siskins. Arriving in large flocks the busy birds descend on the tops of the trees, then move down through the branches in an endless search for insects, spiders and pine nuts, making the tree sing with their humming, buzzing calls. They may hang upside down to get at seeds inside pine cones or to pluck at hard-to-reach treats. Satisfied they have combed one tree thoroughly, the group swirls up out of one tree to the top of another and so moves through the woods.

Siskins have a curious fondness for salt; flocks of them swarm around salt licks, visit docks where fish are cured, or drop onto roads to gather the road salt—a dangerous habit resulting in many run-over siskins.

Instead of settling into defined breeding grounds like many birds, siskins wander about their range as if no breeding imperative controls them. They may breed one year in a certain area and the next somewhere far away. Once the young leave the nest, the flocks of siskins resume their vagabond ways, roaming again far and wide. They frequently pal around in mixed flocks with juncos, redpolls, goldfinches and crossbills.

When and Where to See Them: In mountain pine or spruce forests and mixed woodlands throughout the Rocky Mountain region in summer; lower-elevation shrublands and fields in winter throughout the Rockies except northern Canada.

EYECATCHERS

These familiar, small brown birds flutter about mountain pine forests in typical busy finch fashion. Watch for the flashing of their yellow wing patches as a flock flies overhead.

Pine Siskin

Canada Geese

Index

We encourage you to patronize your local bookstores. Most stores will order any title that they do not stock. You may also order directly from Mountain Press by mail, using the order form provided below or by calling our toll-free number and using your Visa or MasterCard. We will gladly send you a complete catalog upon request.

Some other Natural History titles of interest:

____A Guide to Rock Art Sites Southern California and Southern Nevada	$20.00
____Alpine Wildflowers of the Rocky Mountains	$14.00
____Beachcombing the Atlantic Coast	$15.00
____Birds of the Central Rockies	$14.00
____Birds of the Northern Rockies	$12.00
____Birds of the Pacific Northwest Mountains	$14.00
____Coastal Wildflowers of the Pacific Northwest	$14.00
____Edible and Medicinal Plants of the West	$21.00
____Graced by Pines The Ponderosa Pine in the American West	$10.00
____Hollows, Peepers, and Highlands An Appalachian Mountain Ecology	$14.00
____An Introduction to Northern California Birds	$14.00
____An Introduction to Southern California Birds	$14.00
____The Lochsa Story Land Ethics in the Bitterroot Mountains	$20.00
____Mammals of the Central Rockies	$14.00
____Mammals of the Northern Rockies	$12.00
____Mountain Plants of the Pacific Northwest	$20.00
____New England's Mountain Flowers	$17.00
____Northwest Weeds The Ugly and Beautiful Villains of Fields, Gardens, and Roadsides	$14.00
____Owls, Whoo are they?	$12.00
____Plants of Waterton-Glacier National Parks and the Northern Rockies	$12.00
____Roadside Plants of Southern California	$14.00
____Sagebrush Country A Wildflower Sanctuary	$14.00
____Watchable Birds of the Southwest	$14.00

Please include $3.00 per order to cover shipping and handling.

Send the books marked above. I enclose $_____

Name_____

Address_____

City_____State_____Zip_____

☐ Payment enclosed (check or money order in U.S. funds)
Bill my: ☐ VISA   ☐ MasterCard   Expiration Date:_____

Card No._____

Signature_____

Mountain Press Publishing Company
P.O. Box 2399 • Missoula, MT 59806
Order Toll Free 1-800-234-5308
Have your Visa or MasterCard ready.